A Pianist's Dictionary

Reflections on a Life

Alan Hersh

Hamilton Books
A member of
The Rowman & Littlefield Publishing Group
Lanham • Boulder • New York • Toronto • Plymouth, UK

Hamilton Books
4501 Forbes Boulevard
Suite 200
Lanham, Maryland 20706
Hamilton Books Acquisitions Department (301) 459-3366

Estover Road
Plymouth PL6 7PY
United Kingdom

Printed in the United States of America
British Library Cataloging in Publication Information Available

Library of Congress Control Number: 2009933429
ISBN: 978-0-7618-4838-7 (paperback : alk. paper)
eISBN: 978-0-7618-4839-4

There are many people who have had a big hand in my life and career in music:

My Maternal Grandfather whom I never knew but for whom I'm named.

My other Grandfather who trekked up the elevated steps to take me to my weekly piano lessons at the Juilliard School when I was ten.

My Mother who, despite her reservations, always supported me.

My Father who never had any reservations but a big and cheerful hole in his wallet.

My many colleagues, teachers, friends, and enemies. Piano World can be a brutal place.

Most of all my lifelong friend, companion, teacher, listener, and duo-piano partner: my wife.

Contents

Introduction

When I was a graduate student at Indiana University, I once asked my piano teacher at what tempo to play Schumann's notoriously difficult C Major TOCCATA. My teacher was Sidney Foster, holder of the School of Music's first University Professor rank, and a distinguished pianist and careful thinker.

"I don't know" responded Sidney. "Schumann didn't tell me!"

I've thought about that response during the many intervening years since I left IU to become, in my own small way, a performing pianist, professor, and teacher of music and specifically, of the piano.

At the time, I recognized Sidney's response as more than a clever one-liner. As a teacher, Sidney never ducked the difficult questions, and went out of his way to try to give detailed and reasoned explanations to the many vexing questions that go along with graduate study and with playing the piano.

I knew, from that and many other conversations, that Sidney believed there were no "correct" tempi; that questions of interpretation were really just that; and the successful music performance created a persuasive, sometimes overwhelming sonorous experience from the raw materials of piano sound, dynamic, tempo and balance that were vaguely indicated through an imprecise symbol system we call "music notation."

After my own years of performance and of teaching, I have added yet another few words to this story which I often tell to students. "What is the tempo of Schumann's C Major TOCCATA? I don't know. Schumann didn't tell me, and if he did, I'd probably not pay very much attention."

Schumann, after all, was a notoriously imaginative and, in his later years, unstable musician who, in a famous incident in his youth, wrecked his piano-playing career with an ill-chosen device meant to strengthen one of his weak fingers. His schizophrenic personality changes, revealed so expressively in the imaginative titles and character designations that are found throughout his piano music, only reinforce the impression of a supremely gifted composer who probably changed his mind about tempi three times a day.

But more importantly, I have come to believe that any composer relinquishes control over the performance of her or his compositions the moment a contractual agreement to publish is signed. What composer wants or expects the same response from every member of the audience? Why would the same composer want to limit the creative imagination of a gifted, or even an unimaginative reader and interpreter of the score?

One might assume that one of the most valued attributes of the Arts is the possibility of *CREATIVE AMBIGUITY*, that uncanny possibility for the same performance to elicit vastly different responses from individual listeners in the same audience, or even different responses from the same individual on different occasions of hearing the same music. How often do we return to the same recording and hear it with fresh, or sometimes jaded, senses? Our awareness as listeners to the same recorded performance changes with repeated hearings. Why wouldn't our awareness of notated composition similarly change over time? More importantly, why wouldn't our reading of the same notation be different from that of any other reader?

I once heard a colleague say, in a deprecating manner, that anything played by the great Russian virtuoso Vladimir Horowitz always became Horowitz – Chopin; Horowitz – Liszt; Horowitz – Scriabin. This criticism implied that somehow Horowitz missed the point. Indeed, I believe just the opposite: Horowitz got the point. The score was the beginning, not the end of his imagination, and it was Horowitz' creativity, his insight, his technical ability that made Chopin's score come alive, however different his Chopin might have been from Rubinstein's, Sidney Foster's, or mine. *CREATIVE AMBIGUITY* is what makes the arts meaningful and alive from age to age, from performer to performer, from audience to audience, however much this notion makes some of us uncomfortable.

One can only speculate why this ambiguity, this lack of a fixed or fixable artistic product, makes us so uncomfortable. I suspect that one reason has to do with our human reluctance to live with ambiguities. We like our experiences to be defined, our art experiences to be predictable. Real life is too full of ambiguities and the unexpected. Rather than mirror life, I suspect we'd rather have art experiences that are more definable, more explicable, more closely aligned with the rules of "right" and "wrong."

One can also speculate that the commerce that drives the arts like any other commodity is at the root of an almost theological insistence about "purity of expression." What better way to justify a particular artist than to elevate her or his insight, expressiveness, technical flair, above that of all others? Thus we have Schnabel, the Beethoven specialist; Rubinstein, the

Chopinist; Horowitz, the reincarnation of Liszt; Oppens, the mistress of 20th century style. In no way are these remarks meant to detract from the extraordinary artistry of this distinguished list of pianists, but they are hardly singular in their achievements or insights. Rather, theirs are a few of the reputations elevated to the pianist's "Hall of Fame" by commercial success. Indeed, commerce is itself almost a self-fulfilling prophecy. A particular pianist is given mystical insight or power, his or her interpretation raised to that exalted level of "true to the composer's intentions," and by virtue of media hype, lo and behold, the prophecy is fulfilled until replaced by a newer version.

My first experience as soloist with orchestra came when I was about eighteen, and was mysteriously selected to play Rachmaninov's *Second Concerto* with the Manhattan School Orchestra. At the first rehearsal, the conductor, a famous and somewhat elderly gentleman, immediately achieved the requisite level of intimidation over the callow young student by informing me to "Just pay attention and follow me! I've played this concerto at least a dozen times with Rachmaninov as soloist."

"Ah, yes!" chortled an equally famous member of the piano faculty at lunch soon after when my teacher related the story. "One of these days, I expect a conductor to tell me that he played the Beethoven 'Emperor' with Beethoven as soloist!"

"Creative ambiguity" in the arts is not limited to the score!

All of this is probably amusing, and some among you readers will be nodding your heads in sympathy – or in disapproval. But it is appropriate to ask at this point: "So what's the point?"

"The point" has to do with the intimidation, discomfort, and lack of success that too often attend piano study at all levels. Admittedly, the piano is a difficult instrument to learn, even at the earliest stages. It involves a fairly complicated symbol system called *music notation*; difficult issues of left and right hand, hand/eye, and hand/foot and eye coordination. It obliges the imagination to translate that symbolic notation into living sound, and the discrimination and often a stubborn disposition to make the results conform to a personal view of how the music might sound. When the issues of "right," "wrong," "talent," and other value judgments are added, the pianist can be overwhelmed to the point of frustration and, frequently, failure.

Somewhere is a statistic that suggests over half of the American population at one time or another has had piano lessons. Most discontinue their study after less than three years. Perhaps it is time to reconsider what we mean by "piano study" and its accompanying vocabulary, a language that is often loaded with special meanings and unexamined assertions.

It is for the students, their teachers, and these questions that this volume is intended.

Chapter One

Accompanist

Many years ago, I attended a concert at Orchestra Hall in Chicago. The musicians were perhaps the most famous violinist of the time (name omitted to protect the guilty!), and the pianist Brooks Smith, who was one of the most famous piano collaborators of the time. The program included sonatas by Beethoven and Brahms as well as more conventional works that were meant to display the virtuosity and other skills of the violinist as much as impress us with the inherent artistic worth of the music.

The violinist stood well forward, a few feet from the front of the stage. The pianist was placed almost at the rear of the stage, a visual if not an aural representation of his subordinate role in the proceedings. Paradoxically, the piano has perhaps the dominant role in the Beethoven and Brahms sonata repertoire as musicians well know. It would be appropriate to describe these works as *"concertos"* for two instruments, although *"duo"* will do. But to suggest that the violinist had the leading, dominant role in the proceedings was clearly a deliberate misrepresentation of the aesthetic intent if not the performance reality.

Years later, I asked a colleague, a former student of this violin virtuoso, why his teacher might have arranged things in this manner. "Brooks Smith didn't sell the tickets or fill the hall." was his astute reply.

I have become wary of the label *"accompanist."* The piano has and will continue to fill many roles in the musical firmament. In the music of church and concert hall, in jazz quintet and student all state auditions, in musical theatre and ballet rehearsals, in elevator wallpaper music: the peripatetic piano is always with us. In all these instances, take away the piano (or more recently, the electric keyboard) and what is left?

The piano collaborates and supports, and on many occasions, leads. The sensitive and aware "accompanist" knows when to get out of the way and when to take the lead. In most cases in which it is involved, the piano is something like the central processing unit in the computer. No piano, no music.

"Accompanists" though, have become a self-effacing bunch. I know of one professional accompanist whose constant facial expression resembles more a grimace than the smile of humility he intends to present. It makes him seem non-threatening to the insecure prima donnas who value his services. Many of the beneficiaries of piano collaboration have little or no awareness of the importance of their partner. Unlike the pianist who usually knows the other parts as well as her or his own, musicians who benefit from the pianist's role frequently don't know the piano part and have no interest in knowing it. They are the "star," the reason tickets are sold and audiences attend, and woe be to the pianist who exceeds his or her place in the proceedings. I sometimes think that one of the requisites for success as an accompanist is a willingness to sublimate one's musical personality to that of the other, one reason that piano virtuosos often do not make satisfactory "accompanists." They are too used to asserting their personality and musical ideas to submit to this game of "who's on top."

The best ensembles, of course, are those in which the piano and its partners agree to work as equals, each valuing the rightful importance of the others, each willing to both lead and follow. In these circumstances, "accompanist" is far less useful as a descriptive term than "collaborator" or "partner" but, alas, this happy state is more likely in the abstract than in the real world.

But, pianists can take heart. Some small progress has been made. More often than not these days, the name of the pianist is included in the listing of the performers, usually at the bottom of the program . . . in small print.

Chapter Two

Analysis

The literature of the piano is as complicated as one chooses to make it. Over the years, and usually after the fact, an extensive vocabulary has evolved to help musicians and would-be musicians make sense of what they do and how they might understand the complex semiotic coding that we call music notation. This "deconstruction" of the score is called *Analysis*.

Analyze what? The performance of music involves two distinct but interrelated kinds of understanding. The first has to do with the production of the sounds from which the music is shaped. For pianists, this means some understanding of the piano and its acoustic properties; and more complicated yet, some understanding of the physicality of piano playing. This physicality is usually lumped under the heading of *Technique* and is discussed in some detail in a later entry.

The second kind of understanding tries to make some sense of that semiotic coding we call *Music Notation*. This coding involves matters of pitch, time, and dynamic, and the ways a pianist might order them to produce a performance of the piece of music being considered. The ordering of these factors, based upon one's "analysis" of the "score," is not an idle speculative exercise as some music theorists might suggest, but serves the eminently practical purpose of providing specific ways in which one might turn the printed page into those glorious sound images that make music so compelling to both player and listener.

We often associate this understanding and ordering with the term *Music Theory*, a discipline that is taught at all levels of music study. But there is nothing theoretical about analysis. It helps the pianist uncover the "meaning" that he or she is trying to express through the physical production of sound. *Mindfulness—"analysis"*—at whatever level it is practiced, must precede sound if any performance is to rise above the level of "chance," and while there is a lovely body of music which asks for "chance" as a (non) organizing factor, this is probably not what most of us understand when we sit down to learn a piece of piano music.

The most rudimentary reading of a piece of music immediately establishes some response in us: dramatic, lyric, tedious. To a great extent, our first reading of an unfamiliar piece of music is conditioned by our skill in analysis and our ability to practice the pattern perception we learn by studying Music Theory.

Much of the standard piano repertoire has been recorded and these days, even the materials used in the earliest stages of instruction are increasingly accompanied by a recorded performance of the printed score. Consequently, the "analysis" of music is being more conditioned by the ear than eye and *Imitation* and *Modeling,* based upon what we hear, is or has almost become a substitute for analytic learning. (*Analytic learning* here means the decoding and transformation of the score into a performance.)

This is both good and bad. During the past hundred years or so, music learning was too often an abstract exercise in note reading, and a performance was shaped and directed by a "master" teacher whose decisions were often both unappealing and unappealable. The live performance of a piece of music was infrequent and transitory, and who was to say that the evolving model, controlled by the teacher, could be anything else? The advent of media –radio and particularly of recordings - has completely changed these circumstances and today's aspiring pianist can often find literally dozens of recorded performances upon which to base his or her own conception. I find this circumstance far more appealing than the slavish access to only one teacher's view, but at the same time, there are pitfalls to this approach.

It seems to me that of the many arguments in favor of piano study and piano playing, one of the most compelling is the development of creativity and the ability to mold ambiguity into a persuasive statement. To some extent, any performance of a piano piece is conditioned by the pianist's experience (and technique!) but a pianist's ability to do serious and thoughtful analysis is invaluable in helping foster the skills needed to create a personal statement from the mass of possibilities presented by the score.

What does the pianist/analyst seek? Patterns of melody and harmony; occurrences of repetition and contrast; possibilities for dynamic inflection; and modes of presentation that translate the symbols on the page into a living and affective series of sound images.

The great music theorist Jan La Rue suggests that analysis is about description, not prescription. The analyst is not seeking to find only the stock patterns and predictable occurrences that occupy even the most enlightened theory texts. Rather, the analyst needs be open to possibility, to unusual or even new formulations of familiar symbols, sounds and events. With this openness comes the possibility of an individual reading of even the familiar texts and the renewal of even the most often-performed repertoire.

Historically, it would seem that much of the preceding hundred years of piano study has, at least in theory, paid attention to the creative or at least fundamental application of "analysis" to the study of the piano. Thus, all piano students have had many and often tedious classes in *Music Theory, Harmony,* and *Analysis*. In reality, the content of these courses often was left behind at exit from the classroom and most students found little use or purpose for this study in the real world of making music.

During the sixth and seventh decades of the twentieth century, a movement called *Comprehensive Musicianship* evolved. It was led by a number of theorists and composers who felt that music ought be an integrated series of studies rather than a discrete series of isolated disciplines. *Comprehensive Musicianship* flourished for awhile and several generations of music students seemed to become more aware of the value of studying analysis and composition rather than limiting their creativity to the performance of their instrument in isolation. Sadly, the complexity of organizing, teaching and learning in this fashion eventually sounded its own death knell, and even the advent of computers has not helped significantly in devising a more integrated approach toward music study.

One notes that the study of jazz piano always obliges a "creative" component: composition. Perhaps this is one of the reasons that the study of "jazz performance" with the perception of its inherent emphasis on "personal creativity" is so much more popular than the study of "classical repertoire" with the perception of its slavish replication of "historic convention."

Part of the problem is that analysis needs be creative and needs to lead to a product. Given the possibility of many different readings of the same text – compare a dozen recordings of the same piano piece – it should immediately be apparent that any analysis, like any performance, is neither correct nor incorrect, but rather, compelling, interesting or less interesting. But once again, this creates problems for quantifying judgment in aesthetic matters which often seems the heart of the matter. We prefer having someone else to tell us how to play – in recording, or in the teaching studio – rather than subject ourselves to the discipline, freedom, and often confusion inherent in deciding for oneself.

I am reminded of the unbreakable admonition against the writing of parallel fourths, fifths, and octaves that seemed to be at the heart of counterpoint studies when I was a student. These were rules, not guidelines, and woe be the careless exam taker who was found to have committed this sin on a counterpoint exam. It meant little that we students would often find examples of such parallelisms in the work of the master contrapuntist, Sebastian Bach, and of course, the music of the twentieth century is replete with these deliberate effects. But no matter! It was an accepted part of our training that parallel fourths, fifths and octaves were to be avoided at all costs.

Similarly, woe be to the creative mind that finds a new reading of a familiar work by Chopin, or dares extend pedaling conventions in the keyboard music of Sebastian Bach. Accountability is more easily measured by how many correct notes are played at speed, not the effect of the performance of those notes.

Finally, there seems to be a reaction against "analysis" and the performance of "structure" among the younger generation of pianists. Some of these gifted pianists create puzzlement in the ears and minds of their listeners because of their idiosyncratic readings of familiar music, their stretching of the bounds of conventional analysis. We often don't know what to do with such performers: elevate them to the role of genius or belittle them as undereducated slaves to commercial manipulation and shock value.

The problem with analysis is that at its best, it is singular, and the producers of singular analysis in performance often are like prophets crying out in the wilderness.

Chapter Three

Authenticity

It has always seemed to me that *Authenticity* is the first refuge of scoundrels. While there are many devoted performers, historians, and theorists in the authenticity movement in music, ultimately, I believe those who claim some fundamental insight or truth about the performance of music from earlier (or our) time are deluding either themselves or the unwary who read "scholarly" or other credentials as themselves inerrant. Nothing could be more contentious an assertion. After an initial rush by many musicians and critics (as well as record producers and other commercial enterprises) to climb on board the "authenticity" movement, the more careful appraisal of assertions and performances in recent years seems to be leading to quite different conclusions.

"Bach should not be performed on the piano, the sound was foreign to his ears." "Don't use the damper pedal in the keyboard music of Bach or Scarlatti. The piano should, as much as possible, be made to sound like a harpsichord." "Rubato in Chopin means playing the left hand before the right." "Observe scrupulously the pedal markings in Beethoven." "The *Urtext* is the only acceptable source to use." "Liszt's arrangements of music from other media are meretricious rip-offs."

Bach had no hesitation in transcribing his own music and the music of his peers to his own use. No one would argue that Bach's music, performed on the piano, is not "different" from Bach's music performed on the harpsichord or organ. But to assume that Bach's music should be performed only in the medium for which it was written ignores the practice of Bach himself. Further, for what conceivable purpose, if it were even possible, would one try to recreate the circumstances of time past? The "truth" in an art work is not bounded by geography, history, or personality, but exists primarily in the mind of the person who seeks it. Yes, there is an historical manuscript that was conceived by an historical figure named Sebastian Bach—whoever that was! (The issue of forgery is a fascinating matter but beyond the scope of this discussion)—but we have no way of knowing very much about that document or the mind of its creator. Nor is this knowing of much significance in the performance of a keyboard work of Bach today. It is certainly interesting, as is most historical or theoretical speculation, but to make the leap from speculation to assertion because of the scrupulous attention given documents, commentaries, and other extant materials from the time is not justified or even desirable in my opinion.

Johann Quantz is an often-cited source of musical performance practice in the time of Sebastian Bach. But it seems no more likely that Quantz and his contemporaries were any more accurate about the state of music in their day than Schoenberg, Boulez, or Madonna in ours. "Truth" is in the eye (and mind) of the beholder, and we all see differently.

As to the notion that period instruments, tempi, or intonation should be followed to replicate the sound, mood, or other circumstance of the time, one must again ask the question "Why?" Our time is no better but certainly no worse than earlier times. What do we gain by abandoning our current sensibilities, attitudes, and aesthetic judgment acquired during a lifetime of conditioning, thoughtfulness and contemplation, in an attempt to recapture that mystical and mythical past? Nostalgia is a wonderful and human quality that thrives in our era of plentiful media exposure. Indeed, nostalgia seems to be one of the main themes of our contemporary media. Why not return to that musical Garden of Eden where times were simpler, harmonies unblemished by chromaticism, and rhythm uninfluenced by drum machines and decibels undreamed of even one hundred years ago?

Let us not misunderstand this evocation of a Rousseau-like "noble musical savage". Its products are certainly as viable as commerce and advertising make them, but these products are just that: new wine in old bottles, whose labels make promises that are neither possible nor even desirable.

Bach's music performed on the harpsichord is indeed stimulating, attractive, and often compelling, but no more so than Bach's music performed on the piano by Richter, Gould, or Schiff. Each performance brings its own truth, its own integrity, its own world. None is any more (nor any less) "true" than another. The authentic original died with Bach.

Chapter Four

Competition

I won the first piano competition in which I was entered. I was ten or eleven years old. We, my family and I, lived in Central New Jersey and somehow, I found myself competing in an amateur arts competition at Monmouth Park Racetrack, located just outside of Red Bank. I don't remember any of the details, any of the other competitors, or how or why I participated. I do remember I played Chopin's *REVOLUTIONARY ETUDE* at double tempo and double fortissimo.

I might have had an intuitive understanding that these two qualities—loud and fast—are usually essential if one is to do well in competitions. But intuition aside, a more likely reason for my success was that I simply did not know any better, and while I played everything too loudly and too quickly, these qualities impressed the judges. Add extreme youth to "loud and fast" and you have the ingredients for a winner, yet another veritable "wunderkind."

The judges, whoever they might have been, deemed me the first place winner. In addition to a nice check—my first earnings as a pianist—my family and I were invited to a victory dinner at Asbury Park's Berkeley Carteret Hotel, at that time one of the New Jersey shore's premier establishments. Another young virtuoso was born, hooked by the twin inducements of parental approval and a great after-concert celebration.

It seems to me that there is something contradictory about the avowed purpose of music and of music competitions.

Music purports to elevate our lives and our senses. In the long history of philosophy, many words have been devoted to the moral and ethical value of the arts and of music in particular, with innumerable discussions of the "good" and the "bad" and how one might distinguish between them. While there is scant agreement about which is what, most would suggest that "music" in some fundamental way can be ethical, elevating, spiritual. Indeed, even (or especially) today's most popular musics—rock and rap—affirm their social, aesthetic and moral foundations, even as they seek to maximize sales.

How can we justify music on its ethical or moral grounds if it is simply a matter of who plays the most notes most accurately or quickly? Well, we can judge who plays the most beautifully, the most sensitively, the most insightfully! But when we choose competition winners by these criteria, criteria that are both subjective and impossible to measure, we immediately enter the garden of "taste." Of course, "taste" as we know, is a matter of taste. Piano gymnastics are much less difficult to quantify. A trained judge counts the notes per second, subtracts the wrong ones, gives a small credit for "sensitivity," "musicality," or "musicianship," and adds up the score. And indeed, score cards such as this are commonly used in judging piano competitions, either as an official tally sheet, or as the personal criteria by which judges decide who gets the check and the contract, and who goes back to the practice room.

I remember judging a mid-level piano competition in Tennessee. The victor was to receive an attractive fee for a performance with the local symphony orchestra. The conductor, as is often the case, was ex-officio but retained the right of refusal and final decision.

The second judge was a fine pianist and teacher and, like me, the survivor of numerous competitions.

The two finalists played, respectively, a Mozart concerto and a Prokofiev concerto. My colleague agreed with me: we could not distinguish between the two. Both performances were technically secure and musically compelling. Both pianists had attractive piano tone, impeccable memory, and excellent stage presence. The only difference was in their choice of repertoire.

Normally in such circumstances, Prokofiev wins. We knew this and the conductor made sure to remind us of this as we went through our deliberations. But for once, we pianists both decided that we would not make the obvious judgment, the drama, energy—and lyricism—of Prokofiev over the more subtle sophistication, beauty and elegance of Mozart. We held firm in our insistence that each performance had been equally attractive and by any measure, a "winner." After some dispute, the conductor made an extraordinarily generous offer. He agreed to declare both performances "winners" and find an additional first prize check and date for a performance. We all knew it was the right thing to do.

Competition is extremely human, a fundamental part of our world and culture, but music competition is a far cry from the noble ideals of "art" that we would have music exemplify. Yet, we must have some way of *identifying* the "good, bad and ugly," of separating the "wheat from the chaff." In the piano business these days, competitions have become indispensable to study and success at all levels.

There are several national organizations in the United States whose essential purpose, aside from hosting very expensive parties held at very expensive conventions, is to offer competitions: competitions at the local, state, regional, and finally, the national levels. Students are auditioned and "winners" promoted to the next level. Some students do this sufficient numbers of times with sufficient success and in so many arenas that they can be considered professional participants. Indeed, there is little disagreement that winning enough of these "sporting events" is one of the few ways most pianists have of establishing some kind of career.

Some of the most vocal critics of this system are precisely the pianists who train the winners and judge the competitions. They frequently decry the uniformity of performances, the accurate but "safe" interpretations, the arbitrary and unfair decisions which send many a worthy performer home before the final round. They offer up many recommendations for change and improvement, yet the competitions continue and if anything, seem to be proliferating. *International Piano Competitions* are expensive to run, but the prestige and commerce that attends one of these events seems to justify the expense and organization.

Piano competitions are not limited to the professional and semi-professional pianist, however. Many a competition is restricted to beginners or intermediate level students. Age limits are scrupulously defined and other boundaries set to level the playing field. But woe be the competitors when some young genius—read "motivated, talented, well taught, and well practiced"—enters the lists. One solution to this phenomenon is the practice of giving all the participants some kind of award, a judges commentary, or other recognition that their hard work is not in vain. They have some tangible proof of achievement beyond the transitory satisfaction of playing a piece of music as well as they are able. Everyone is a winner, even if they and we know that there really are "winners" and "others," at least as defined by our culture—and the competition.

If this competition system of screening the "fit" from the "unfit" seems rather like that of athletics, it is. I'm not sure which sport—music or athletics—has learned from the other. Certainly, professional music competitions are as old as professional sports events—one need only consult classic Greek literature with its poetry and singing contests as well as its javelin throwing and running events—for parallels to contemporary sporting events. But in more recent times, sport has refined its ability to identify and train those seemingly most adept and likely to succeed at the next level, and I suspect that the piano business with its competitions imitates the tactics and methods of those other, more physically oriented entertainment spectacles.

Some might question this parallelism, but it is an open secret that to win one of the "major" piano competitions—the *Van Cliburn* in Texas or the *Tchaikovsky* in Russia, for example—you had better play one of the "big"concertos, most often the Rachmaninov *THIRD* or the Tchaikovsky *Bb MINOR*. The spectacle of heroic soloist battling the orchestral masses while climbing one of the Mount Everests of the concerto repertoire engages the judges in ways that concertos of Mozart or Ravel do not. This entertaining phenomenon is precisely akin to scoring more points or running more quickly than anyone else.

There is an exhilaration in hearing these exhibitions, and one can indeed label them "esthetically uplifting," but they are a far cry from the more neutral aesthetic high ground of meaning and relevance that classical, indeed, most music, would like to claim for itself.

In its most fundamental sense, sports and music are all in the same business: entertainment! *GO BIG RACH!*

Chapter Five

Concert Pianist

A *CONCERT PIANIST* is a person who plays the piano in a concert.

CONCERT PIANISTS come in all nationalities, ages, competencies, sizes, and of course, both genders. For many years, I had a theory that the greatest concert pianists were usually of short stature: 5 feet 8 inches or less. Artur Rubinstein, Josef Lhevine, and Sidney Foster come to mind. But I knew this was simply not true. Sergei Rachmaninov and Jorge Bolet, both well over six feet tall, easily refuted this notion.

Similarly, when I was a student, the idea that men somehow brought some special gender qualification to the life was yet another manifestation of the sexist society that was culturally institutionalized until late in the twentieth century. Men were thought to be more emotionally and physically able to withstand the rigors of concert life, and were more psychologically attuned to making a career. Teresa Carreno, Guiomar Novaes, Gena Bachauer, and Rosalyn Tureck are only a few of the names that belie this bit of harmful nonsense. It is true that for much of the nineteenth and twentieth centuries there were more male than female professional pianists who had big careers and earned a good wage, but recent scholarship has demonstrated that far more women than men played the piano during this time, and a woman's difficulty in establishing a professional career was the consequence of institutionalized sexism, not any particular genetic endowment.

The same might be said of national origins. Many of the great pianists of the late nineteenth century were Russian Jews, but to suggest that this was the result of anything but cultural circumstance is nonsense. In the twentieth century, we have had the emergence of many outstanding pianists with Asian origins, but successful African and Middle Eastern pianists are scarce on the international scene, only because there is less opportunity for the many potentially gifted students in these cultures.

Training for the concert stage is rigorous, time consuming, and single-minded. Training is also expensive and excellent instruction is imperative if the young pianist is to develop skills that are far more sophisticated than might seem apparent. The sixteen year old prodigy who makes a dramatic last minute appearance with the New York Philharmonic, as did Andre Watts, is the product of years of diligent practice and careful oversight by a number of experienced and knowledgeable teachers. There is a familiar musician's anecdote about the parents of an eight year-old who go to a famous piano teacher and say they'd like their child to become a concert pianist. "Too late!" says the teacher. "He should have started five years ago!"

The glamour of the concert pianist's life is probably exaggerated, although there is no shortage of young musicians who enter the lists. After a lengthy period of study, practice, and apprenticeship, a fortunate few begin to tour. Charles Rosen, in his wonderfully appealing book *THE WORLD OF THE PIANIST*, speaks of a seemingly unending series of sterile hotel rooms, meals at odd hours, constant practice and preparation, less-than-satisfactory pianos and audiences, and long journeys to the next concert, where the whole process is repeated. After a few years, most successful pianists are as interested in survival as glamour.

There is a whole subculture of pianists, however, who would willingly sell their souls for the opportunity. These might euphemistically be called "the ones who didn't make it."

There are far fewer opportunities for a pianist to earn a living as a performer than there are pianists who would like to earn their living as performers. Consequently, there are numbers of us who teach in private or public studios, staff college and university faculties, or engage in many other activities to support our habit: the playing of concerts. We play sporadically, often, occasionally, sometimes well, sometimes poorly. We play in under-heated church halls, over-heated school auditoriums, and everywhere else where a piano can be found, imported and tuned (not always.) We are sometimes paid for our efforts, occasionally well, often a pittance, and after the concert, we return to our practice to prepare for the next one, filling the intervening days and hours with the other work by which we earn our daily bread.

Many of us give up the life in middle age. I recently had a conversation with a colleague in her early forties who has been playing and teaching for about twenty years. She is a fine pianist, well trained, imaginative, and industrious, and is thinking of accepting an offer to teach at a larger school despite the dislocation for her life and family. The salary would probably be less, the security of tenure questionable. Why would she consider such a move? "I'd really like to be paid something for my playing." This from a pianist who is a competition winner, and recently played with several orchestras outside the United States. She hopes that teaching at a larger and more prestigious school will help her to secure better paying concerts. Not likely! The well-paying performance careers are mostly spoken for by the age of twenty or twenty-one.

This story is hardly unique. It could be repeated many times over with small variation. The attraction of the piano and of playing piano concerts is considerable, sufficient not only to lure the unwary young person, but to keep the more worldly returning to the stage time and again, despite the hardships and frustrations. The state of the concert piano business says a great deal about economics and the culture in which we live, but also something about the people who continue to practice a profession that has always been precarious and is hardly viable in the modern world.

Our profession is not so different from the world of athletes. Only a few athletes earn their livelihood as players. Most are destined for the extensive network of careers that surround their central passion. They coach, become teachers, administrators. But unlike athletes, our culture, when it attends at all, does not give much credence to concert pianists, and when it does, rarely gets it right. Films such as *THE COMPETITION* or *RHAPSODY* are entertaining and amusing but unlike any reality we have known. Music in our culture is becoming more marginalized as the technology becomes more advanced. Personality, always the cash machine of our advertising, is about the only way to promote a career, and even the most outrageous salesmanship today is often not sufficient to stem the tide of economic history.

It may be that we have entered a new age of patronage, with the public concert no longer economically sustainable and the life of the concert pianist redefined. Even the most successful professionals today take teaching positions in academia, some as artists-in-residence, many as teachers helping to prepare the next generations of young pianists for careers that don't exist.

One can only hope that the major institutions who have assumed the role of patrons—the colleges, universities, schools and churches—continue to support the profession and its practitioners, recognizing that the concert pianist is the keeper of an honorable and historic artistic tradition. But in my subconscious, I keep hearing the voice of that great comic actor Danny DeVito, giving a memorable speech about buggy whips in the film *OTHER PEOPLE'S MONEY*. The best buggy whip factory ever to produce the best buggy whips was developed just about the time the automobile became all the rage.

One can only hope that the concert pianist is not working in that buggy whip factory.

Chapter Six

Concert

We use the term *CONCERT* today to describe a variety of events in which people come together to hear music. The earliest public concerts in Europe date from the later seventeenth century but there is little question that this kind of event, whatever it was called, has been around much longer.

The term *CONCERT* still has references to both "consonance" and "together." In both these meanings, it is implied that "community" is at the heart of the matter: a "community" of musicians performing for a "community" of listeners.

The term *RECITAL* sometimes is used interchangeably with *CONCERT*. Today, we often associate "recital" with fewer performers than "concert" although in current usage, there doesn't seem any clear-cut distinction. But I've never heard anyone say they were going to a rock or jazz "recital,' so perhaps these terms are most often associated with "classical" music performances.

CONCERT is usually preceded by another qualifier such as *CHAMBER*, *SOLO*, *PIANO*, or *ROCK*. Again, the word *CONCERT* is so inclusive that we frequently feel the need to be more explicit about the style of music or the number of performers.

Concerts function as more than entertainment. For performers, they are both personal expression and an important source of compensation, whether or not admission is charged. Patrons of concerts, whether private or public, use concerts to publicize agendas, to advertise their wealth or position, to gather persons together to engender a sense of community. The Fourth of July musical celebrations throughout the United States and annual *Messiah* sings are only two obvious examples of this fostering of community.

But money is at the root of many if not most concert activities. In the classical music world, the public concert and its many offshoots became big business in the nineteenth century and during the twentieth, became a major commercial enterprise. Performers, managers, publicists, and concert hall staff all reaped the benefits of this economic music boom, a boom that was not limited only to large population centers. Almost every small town in America in the time before television had its Community Concert or Visiting Artist Series. These series provided a fundamental source of exposure and opportunity for any number of musicians and a financial basis for the industry.

The history of the public concert is the history of increasing audience size, with consequences for the style of music being written and the instruments upon which it was played. Music with wider ranges of dynamic, varieties of timbre, numbers of players. Music that was tuneful, memorable, with affecting harmonies and lots of contrast. Music that would catch the ear and imagination of ever larger audiences, audiences with disposable income to spend and time to spare.

The piano for many years was an essential part of this enterprise. There is only one player to be paid in the solo piano concert. As the instrument became technologically more developed, its became capable of greater sonority and more contrast, and was able to be heard comfortably in larger and larger spaces. It was a lot cheaper to produce a piano concert than an opera or orchestra performance, and the profits proportionally could be much greater. Mass manufacturing meant that the piano became a familiar commodity to millions of owners, and also assured a greater and greater supply of instruments of proven quality to meet both private and public demand.

The piano, in partnership with instruments or with voice, similarly became an important source of economic plenty for its public performers for many years. Despite some overlap, pianists more and more began to specialize as soloists, as chamber performers, as accompanists. The apprenticeship was long and demanding, but for many pianists, there was a pot of gold awaiting them at some point in their career as a public performer.

The advent of recordings, of television, and of electronic amplification changed the whole piano concert business.

Recordings initially were not as satisfying as live performances and probably encouraged prospective audiences to attend concerts to hear the real thing. But as recording fidelity improved, editing created a performance standard impossible to meet in live performance. Further, it has become a truism that television has changed the communal gathering habits in our culture and the traditional piano recital, unfortunately, is not a good candidate for television broadcasts. Fewer and fewer persons have chosen to attend live piano concerts in recent years and the declining numbers of paying audiences mean fewer and fewer solo piano concerts and fewer and fewer live concerts in which the piano is an important partner. At the beginning of the twentieth-first century, the concert which prominently features the piano is often not economically viable, even for many of the performers who have reached the highest levels of their profession.

Further, the community of audience, when it doesn't stay home to watch television, has now gravitated toward the much larger gatherings of concerts made possible by amplification and electronic means. An average concert of contemporary music—rock, folk, jazz, famous personality—can now be held in a space that accommodates one hundred thousand persons and more and a new aesthetic and musical concert culture has evolved. Alas, the poor acoustic piano. It can often be seen at one of these performances, along with a variety of electronic keyboards, but its viability is dependent upon amplification. Indeed, aside from the visual appearance of the acoustic piano, its role in this contemporary concert culture can better be fulfilled by any number of electronic keyboards and the days of the acoustic piano as a participant in these concerts is probably numbered.

A few words about concert costumes and etiquette are in order. The dress of concert performers can range from archaic formal wear to comfortable casual. There is always an important element of theatre in any concert, and the costume of the performers helps define the parameters of both the performer and the music. It is a visual clue to the audience about how to respond.

Audiences often sit silently through the most tedious formal classical concerts, afraid even to cough for fear of violating the ethos of the moment. Similarly, audiences are encouraged not to applaud, except at appropriately sanctified moments in the proceedings. The argument for this behavior is that the audience should be so involved in following the narrative thread and intellectual affect of the music that applause would intrude on this attentiveness and ruin the moment. In reality, many members of a classical concert audience don't have a clue about what is going on, and would probably be happier were their behavior less restricted, as is the norm in more contemporary concert settings. But classical concert audiences have been replicating church behavior for centuries and to suggest that their behavior be less formal might loose the tenuous hold that performers occasionally have on their audience.

The exception to this behavior is the occurrence of a truly remarkable virtuoso performance. At such a concert, the audience throws formality to the wind to cheer, stamp, and whistle. This spontaneous eruption is usually greeted by the performer(s) humble acknowledgment, a kind of "Ah, shucks, twern't nothin" kind of behavior which performers sometimes practice as much as their performance. Perhaps loosening the restrictions might indeed be a good thing, perhaps not?

Chapter Seven

Dynamics

Dynamics are the heart and soul of expressiveness on the modern acoustic piano.

The idea and production of the earliest pianos has been credited to an Italian harpsichord craftsman, Bartolomeo Cristofori. I've always thought it no accident of geography that the piano was conceived and first produced in Italy. Italian music has a tradition of beautiful singing and its extraordinary extant vocal repertoire dates to before the thirteenth century. This music has always seemed to emphasize tonal beauty, expressiveness, the communication of emotion through music. Even the Italian language, by its structure and sound, seems particularly suited to lend itself to beauty of expression.

DYNAMIC VARIETY is at the heart of all musical expressiveness in our tradition, the rise and fall of melody, the constant interplay of loud and soft sounds that beguiles or sometimes overwhelms the mind as it leads it now here, now there.

The human voice is often characterized as the most perfect instrument for expression but the human voice has some built in limitations. Singers have a range of about fifteen notes, they get tired, they run out of breath, sometimes in the middle of an idea.

In my mind, Cristofori was interested in attempting to marry the technology of the keyboard instruments of his time, particularly the harpsichord, with the dynamic inflection and expressiveness of the human voice. From all accounts a progressive thinker and an unusually competent keyboard engineer, Cristofori was undoubtedly intrigued by the possibilities of that emerging culture we now call the *ENLIGHTENMENT*: the perfectibility of the world through the application of technology. It's not only that Cristofori had the technical skills that led to his invention of the first "pianos." It seems to me that Cristofori, like many skilled engineers of his time and later, believed in the possibilities of technological innovation and believed he could apply his skills to improving upon the limitations of the human voice. In this marriage of technology and biology, it seems to me that we find a model of that most modern of attitudes: we can improve upon nature if we're clever enough. "Progress" through innovation!

Christofori described his new and hybrid instrument as a "keyboard instrument that could play both soft (piano) and loud (forte)." As an instrument, it was an idea whose time had come, although the earliest pianos resemble the modern versions only in their most fundamental conception and appearance. The instrument that we currently recognize as the "modern" acoustic piano was really not produced until the last part of the nineteenth century, and even today, small adjustments in engineering and manufacture continue. (For a complete discussion of the history of the acoustic piano, readers are referred to the classic *GIRAFFES, BLACK DRAGONS, AND OTHER PIANOS* by Edwin M. Good.)

Christofori's invention spread rapidly and by the beginning of the nineteenth century, the piano was becoming a staple of European and American musical culture although it still shared the home or stage with the harpsichord. The mighty organ, the king of instruments then as now, held sway in the churches and cathedrals, but the much smaller pianos were recognized early on as great accompanists and rehearsal tools by musicians.

Because of its long period of development—about one hundred and fifty years from conception to finished design—the piano's dynamic contrast and inflection that was understood and essential to the compositional style of the classic composers was different from the dynamics we expect and can achieve with the modern piano. Mozart, Haydn, Beethoven, even Chopin and Liszt wrote for an instrument significantly different from the modern instrument. Here lies the root of a modern interpretative dilemma: does the modern pianist deliberately limit the dynamic range of music from earlier times, or does the modern pianist adapt his or her interpretative impulse to the instrument upon which she or he plays?

Further, we also understand that concert rooms and their acoustic properties have a significant impact on dynamics. Before the mid-nineteenth century, rare was the hall that seated more than a few hundred persons. Smaller sounds, smaller range of dynamics, smaller spaces to fill. What is a modern pianist to do?

Each player must decide for herself or himself the solution that satisfies their artistic impulse. Some prefer limited dynamics and a small range of sounds. Some choose maximum dynamic contrast and maximum sound production. Pick your poison.

Further complicating the issue of dynamic variety and expressiveness is the almost complete monopoly that recorded performance currently has in the world of piano music. Anyone who has seen the technological sophistication of a modern recording studio with its multi—microphone pickups and mixing boards recognizes that dynamic variety and acoustical fidelity are almost totally at the discretion of the recording engineer. The products of this technology—the recordings—bear little resemblance to the live acoustical experiences that include the modern piano, and those who develop their sound and dynamic concepts exclusively from recordings are learning to hear and expect a sound unlike any they will experience in a live acoustical setting. Ironically, more often than not, modern recording engineers seem to prefer the clean if somewhat bland sound of *TERRACED DYNAMICS* and engineers have been known to deliberately override the variety of dynamic choices offered by a sensitive pianist in the studio. "Terraced" levels of dynamic more closely resemble the dynamic characteristics of the harpsichord than the subtle inflections that can characterize performances on the modern piano and in some sense, recordings sometimes seem to be returning to the dynamic ideals that prompted Christofori to begin his experiments.

What goes 'round comes 'round!

Chapter Eight

Expressiveness

Expressiveness is in the mind of the beholder.

The tools of expressiveness in piano playing are:

Dynamics: loud, soft, or getting louder or softer, which in music we call crescendo or diminuendo- dynamic inflection.

Time: fast and slow (tempo); or getting faster or slower; or lingering; or simply playing out of time and freely; or playing strictly in time with an emphasis upon accurate presentation of meter and pattern.

BALANCE or *VOICING*: when two or more simultaneously occurring sounds are playing, the degree to which one of the sounds is "highlighted" or stands out compared to the others.

There is also a "visual" expressiveness in piano playing, what I like to describe as the "theatrics" of performance. Some pianists sit quietly with little or no body movement; others prefer to rock and roll, fling their hands, and indulge in various facial grimaces and even grunts to convey their reaction to what they are doing. With the increasing prominence of visual images of piano performances, "theatre" is becoming an important component of expressiveness, the performer's visual cue to how the listener might respond.

EXPRESSIVENESS is a consequence of both intuition and modeling. Most persons who begin the process of translating musical notation to sound immediately begin to arrange the sounds in some order that satisfies their idea of musical expressiveness, however simple it might be. Clearly, some beginning pianists are more creative, intuitive, aggressive, or adept at doing this. I believe this is one of the qualities we describe as *TALENT*, that is, the ability to imitate persuasively, intuitively. But despite intuition or talent and however limited in effect, it is not possible to play the piano without attempting some kind of expressiveness.

I would describe *MODELING* as the attempt to imitate a performance that the pianist finds expressive. The model might be a teacher, a recording, or a live performance. The model need not be only the piece being studied or even in a familiar style. Rather, we learn general modes of expressiveness from all kinds of music. Our experience and our personal notions of expressiveness are a kind of pick and choose from the effects we've heard and want to reproduce.

Dynamic, Time, Voicing - the possibilities in a piece of music are almost endless and give us the opportunity to discover what is creative in our own psyches. While there are expressive conventions associated with various styles, with composers, and even with specific pieces of music, one of the immense satisfactions of playing the piano is to explore one's personal ideas, even as one develops more sophisticated tactics and concepts. Expressiveness is never static in a pianist but grows with experience, perspective, and personality. Our ideas of expressiveness change over the years, and one of the unexpected pleasures of growing older with the instrument and its music is the subtle nuance that one begins to understand as "expressiveness" in piano playing.

However, one unfortunate consequence of strongly held beliefs about expressiveness is the varying degrees of intolerance for another pianist's playing that we perceive as lacking in our expressive concepts or sophistication. This intolerance seems to increase with age and perhaps helps explain why so many senior piano teachers are so crotchety and opinionated: they grow exasperated at not hearing the expressive playing they anticipate and know to be correct.

Perhaps older teachers should only have older students.

Chapter Nine

Fingering

The human hand was not intended to play the piano. With its opposing thumbs and differing finger lengths and strengths, the physical act of piano playing requires some conscious adaptation of the hand to the geography of the keyboard and the requirements of its music.

I once knew a very fine teacher who was also a very fine pianist. In a tragic, if all too common disaster, he had lost two fingers from his left hand during the Second World War. Somehow, this artist had found ways of fingering and arranging his left-hand parts so that a casual listener probably would not know they were listening to an eight-fingered pianist.

There are no easy rules or guidelines for choosing fingering in piano music. Frequently, the most confusing place to begin is the score, where editors sometimes mark fingerings that are nonsensical or downright impossible. For this reason alone, a good edition is worth the extra money it often costs. Carefully chosen fingerings by a competent editor will help any pianist learn to play more effectively. Poorly chosen fingerings almost always lead to disaster. It is especially unfortunate that the most usual victims of poorly fingered piano music are the least experienced players who look at anything on the printed page as holy writ, and frequently cannot play a piece or even a passage because of trying to follow printed fingerings.

It is worth emphasizing: good fingering choices are essential to playing a piano piece. Editors are paid to edit. Many take their responsibility seriously, but editing is a difficult and complex task, and just because finger numbers appear extensively in printed piano music is no guarantee they are good choices! For example, editors with large hands might well choose fingerings that are problematic for pianists with small hands, and vice versa.

The pianist's fingers are numbered 1 through 5 with the thumb of each hand #1 and the small finger #5. If you spread your hands flat on a table, it is immediately apparent that the thumbs are adjacent and the small fingers farthest away. The hands are mirror images of each other. That is, your hands are opposites and are attached "backwards." This can be a significant problem in playing music that moves in the same direction in both hands simultaneously: the hands are using completely different fingers to play patterns moving in the same direction.

Consider, for example, a scale in which the hands play together, first in ascending and than in descending motion. This can be a major coordination problem, since your fingers are asked to follow completely different patterns.

RH 1 2 3 1 2 3 4 5
LH 5 4 3 2 1 3 2 1

It is much easier to play in contrary rather than similar or parallel motion. Read the right hand forwards and the left hand backwards to see exactly what this means in this example. This is why knowledgeable teachers begin scale study with contrary rather than similar motion, but also why scale and arpeggio study in similar motion is so useful. Your hands need to become as independent as possible. This means that the part of your brain that controls hand movement is like a split screen TV, with two images being processed simultaneously.

I believe that comfort and ease are essential when choosing fingering. All hands are different sizes and we all have different physical coordination. A simple fingering for one pianist is impossible for another.

To begin developing a theory of fingering, one must begin with the hand: large or small; flexible or stiff; rounded fingers or flat; good extension between fingers or fingers close together. Know your hand, what it can do, what it might do, and what it can't do.

It is often necessary to rearrange or omit notes for smaller hands. In my opinion, it is far preferable to omit notes than to consistently play incorrectly because the hand is too small—or too large. Surprisingly, pianists with large hands often have as much problem with fingering as do those with small.

Try to find a fingering that keeps the hand in balance, with the weight of the hand leaning slightly toward the outside or weak fingers. Some fingerings initially may seem bizarre but ultimately are much easier than conventional choices.

One of my favorite examples of this is the fingering for the major and minor triad in root position. Given a choice, students almost always use 5/3/1/ in the left hand or 1/3/5 in the right. For even a normal teenage hand, this fingering invariably forces a cramming together of the fingers and puts all the weight on the thumb or third finger. Good tone—*VOICING*—would suggest that the weight be on the top note of the triad, and those students who try to balance this chord with fingers 1/3/5 invariably have a difficult time.

Try 4/2/1 in the left hand or 1/2/4 in the right. Immediately, the problem is solved with the weight automatically shifted to the top of the hand and the "pinching" together of the hand eliminated. This is the kind of "unorthodox" fingering that can frequently lead to improved efficiency and ease of playing. (Small hands, of course, do not have this problem!)

Jazz pianists, unhampered by fingering orthodoxy, often are imaginative in finding effective fingerings for the many unusual patterns that they play.

Don't always think adjacent fingers. Remember that "4" can follow "2" as easily as "3" follows "2", and if there is a skip of a third, it makes more sense in terms of hand balance to play 2/4 rather than 2/3.

The distance between the thumb and second finger is far greater than the distance between other finger adjacencies such as two and three, or three and four, and whenever possible, keyboard distances larger than a minor third should be avoided between adjacent fingers not involving the thumb.

Again, think balance, comfort, and where the hand naturally falls rather than adjacent fingers just because they come next.

Sebastian Bach is credited with advising against putting thumbs on black notes in scale passages. This is still sound advice. Remember to pass the thumb under and try to avoid the thumb on black keys, especially in scale passages.

Plan a fingering and write it in the score. When we sight-read a piano piece, we either follow the fingering marked by the editor, or grab whatever finger is available. This is fine for reading when continuity is more important than accuracy, but when we set out to learn a piece fluently, PLAN THE FINGERING and write it in the book. This doesn't necessarily mean the obvious places where it is clear what fingers to use. It does mean those passages or chords where some choices are necessary to achieve fluency.

Learn the conventional scale, chord and arpeggio fingerings. Any reliable piano technique book will give these fingerings and being fluent with these conventional fingerings will go a long way toward providing a basic repertoire of patterns and fingerings that occur over and again in music. The time invested in mastering these conventional fingerings will be repayed immeasurably and make for a much happier and successful playing experience.

Remember to choose a fingering that will work in the correct tempo. Many pianists work out an acceptable fingering at a slow practice tempo and discover it is inadequate for the faster performance tempo.

Also remember that all piano music is not comfortable and some pieces do not lie well for the hand. Don't take fingering for granted. If there is a secret to effective pianism, it is in the choice of appropriate fingering. Fingering choices reflect an awareness of one's hands, an awareness of fingering conventions, and thoughtful choices in solving and thus mastering patterns that are difficult to execute. Fingering is not automatic, and the time initially spent in working out your appropriate fingering for a piano piece will ultimately make learning the piece more pleasurable and successful.

"A fingering in time saves nine!"

Chapter Ten

Improvisation

I think that one of the dreams that lurks in every pianist's heart is the desire to be able to sit down and create a piano piece spontaneously. Even a relative novice can make something up on the spur of the moment, but somehow, most of us never sound quite like those great jazz pianists with their seemingly infinite imagination for spontaneously created piano music.

A well-known piano story has Vladimir Horowitz, one of the greatest virtuosos of all, going to New York jazz clubs to hear Art Tatum play. Horowitz, a composer himself, had the greatest admiration for Tatum, not only as a pianist, but as one of the greatest jazz improvisers, a seemingly endless source of dazzling pianistic imagination and ingenuity.

It's not enough to have the desire in our heart: it also has to be in our head.

The word *IMPROVISATION* is somewhat misleading. Webster's New World Dictionary, Second College Edition defines *IMPROVISE* as: "To compose, or simultaneously compose and perform, on the spur of the moment and without any preparation; extemporize."

While Tatum's dazzling piano improvisations were extemporized, improvisation is anything but unprepared. Great improvisers are actually composers. They spend countless hours working on melodic and harmonic patterns, developing riffs and gestures in many keys and in many permutations. The amount of musical material carried around in a great improviser's mind is sufficient to cause brain overload for most of us.

Sometimes they write these improvisations down. More often, they commit them to memory, and are able to summon them forth, in entirety or in parts, at a moment's notice, to combine and recombine into innovative new compositions—"improvisations." The music exists in the unconscious and frequently, the semi-conscious part of the pianist's brain. Its utterance into new combinations is a seemingly spontaneous act, although all improvisers follow some structural plan, however indefinite. *BLUES IN Eb* may seem pretty vague to the uninitiated, but to an improviser, it's an invitation to summon forth a wealth of previously imagined musical combinations.

There are other ways of playing the piano than the written page.

Historically, keyboard players have always been improvisers. The great organ traditions of the Renaissance and Baroque were based upon improvisation, and it is no coincidence that Buxtehude, Bach, Handel and the young Mozart were also counted as the greatest improvisers of their day. Later, Beethoven made his early career on the strength of his improvisations, as did Chopin, Liszt, and countless other keyboard players who were expected to be able to extemporize as well as compose and perform. While publishing made it possible for musicians to sell their musical ideas and perhaps earn a small living as entrepreneurs, I suspect it also sounded the death knell for the great tradition of classical improvisation. It remained for the newer style of *Jazz* to once again encourage the art of improvisation. It is no coincidence that the early jazz musicians were often unable to read or write music using conventional notation. Instead, their music publishing was through recordings, a new way of documenting musical genius to a new and changing culture.

I've always felt that much of the great keyboard music of the past was simply improvisation that got written down and edited to reflect a final polish by the composer. Indeed, in an opposite process, many of the great jazz improvisations of the past are being transcribed from recordings today, enriching the keyboard literature.

These modern jazz transcriptions in no way diminish the originals. Rather, our admiration for the creative minds that invented these "compositions" is all the greater, because they were done without the benefit of written editing. Editing, of course, allows a "get it right polish" on the part of the composer. Improvisation is of and for the moment!

All pianists can learn to improvise. They just need to work at it.

In my years as a teacher, I've come to believe that there are two kinds of piano student: those who improvise and those who don't. The improvisers often have a difficult time mastering the intricacies of the printed score. The score readers are usually afraid to venture into the uncharted waters of the imaginary and improvised. The ideal teacher would encourage students to explore both worlds.

Performers of the printed page would benefit from the freedom of spontaneous improvisation, the ability to translate the printed page into a seemingly extemporized rather than a studied performance. The natural improviser similarly would benefit from access to the treasures of the piano literature that have been written out and collected for literally hundreds of years. Much of this literature is currently available on recording, but listening to a recording is different from studying and playing through a score.

In all things, balance and moderation!

Chapter Eleven

Lesson

"Do I have to?" pleads the victim.

"It's time for your lesson!" exclaims the voice of authority: parent or conscience.

The moments of truth, the moments for which one has practiced—or not—since the last *LESSON*.

We actually learn to play the piano by *PRACTICING* the piano. Lessons are those places where we get direction for what and how to practice. We hope the giver of the lesson is a voice of wisdom who guides us wisely and with direction. But whatever the skills of the teacher, the lesson is centered about us, what we know, what we've learned, what we need to learn.

Piano lessons have a privileged place in our educational scheme. When piano lessons were the privilege of the aristocracy, piano lessons were often leisurely and social affairs. The young Mozart would arrive at the appropriate palace, listen to the lesson, offer some comments, perhaps a new concerto or two, and be on his way until the next time, somewhat richer than when he came. Lessons have always been a fundamental source of a musician's income, even unto the present day but piano lessons and their associated expenses—piano, music, piano teacher—are a luxury not available to all.

When I was a young student in my mid-teen years, I was the circuit rider kind of piano teacher. While not exactly in Mozart's class, either in terms of talent or compensation, I made a very tidy living going from student home to student home. I was self employed, paid my own expenses, and probably had more wealth than ever again in my life! A few years later, I became a piano lesson subcontractor for a very fine private academy in one of America's wealthiest suburbs. Again, travel from home to home, schedule and route arranged by the directors of the school. Again, a very attractive living teaching the children of

America's aristocracy something about music and something about playing the piano.

Today, more often than not, the piano teacher has given up being a circuit rider and students usually come to the teacher's studio—a home, furnished office, or a "music school" if the teacher is enterprising and resourceful in finding students, and students are usually not difficult to find! Despite large numbers of persons who offer piano lessons, often as an avocation, there always seems to be a waiting list of prospective students eager to study and learn to play.

Most students have no professional aspirations. Many parents do. Usually, parents can be disabused of their ambition before any harm is done. The majority of piano students today want to learn to read music and to play some of the contemporary repertoire they hear on recordings or see on TV. The piano teacher will try to find some compromise between what the teacher is accustomed to teaching and what the student wants to study. Sometimes this is not possible, and in these circumstances, there is an inevitable falling out.

Many piano lessons include studies in music theory. Some teachers also teach the physicality of piano playing–technique. Most teachers also have some kind of performance opportunity as a periodic outcome of study. These include the semi-annual *RECITAL*, usually in a rented church or school hall; the *PERFORMANCE CLASS* for other students or parents; the *MASTER CLASS* with commentary by an invited expert; and the ultimate terror, the *COMPETITION*, either for a gold cup or other trophy or occasionally, for a cash prize and an opportunity for fame and fortune.

Some teachers include competitions as a matter of course in their student's study. Other teachers avoid these events at all cost, fearing negative rather than positive outcomes for their students. While the student is the focus of piano lessons, these performance venues are often decided by the needs of the teacher or the perceived needs of the parents. After all, that loving cup with the bust of Beethoven, awarded after a hard year's study and practice, is as substantial testimony to virtue as the bumper sticker proclaiming "My child is an Honor Student at Such and Such School."

Piano lessons, for the most part, remain singular affairs, the teacher and one student. Lesson times are usually thirty or forty-five minutes weekly. The sixty-minute lesson signals an advanced or potentially serious student—or teacher. More than one sixty minute lesson a week is unusual.

Individual lessons are a luxury for the student and a hardship for the teacher. Because of economic reality, a teacher who is earning his or her livelihood from piano lessons usually has to teach many individual lessons to be viable. I once had a student who taught seventy-five half-hour lessons weekly. Since most piano students in the United States take lessons primarily after school and on Saturdays, this teacher was cramming lessons into every available time slot. She began at seven in the morning on most weekdays and frequently completed her work after nine in the evening. Saturday was an all day affair. Despite this horrendous number of individual lessons, she still taught less than a forty hour work week, at least on paper. Her annual income was not unattractive, but earned at what personal cost! Seventy-five classes a week, seventy-five student personalities, seventy-five lesson plans! Fortunately, this teacher gave up some of the hours after a few years to retain her sanity.

Another teacher I knew taught a large number of individual lessons for three consecutive weeks, but every fourth week gathered her students into groups of ten or fifteen, to play for each other and be a bit more social. This meant that every fourth week, she had a sharply reduced teaching schedule and the students had a different lesson experience. Everyone seemed pleased with the arrangement, and I am not aware that this teacher was any less effective in getting the job done. I've always thought this was a very practicable and intelligent compromise between the individual and group lesson.

GROUP LESSONS have gained a great deal of popularity in recent years with the advent of electronic keyboards. These keyboards are far more space efficient than even the smallest acoustic piano, and a teacher can often fit eight or ten keyboards into a studio. With headphones plugged in to keep the din at a manageable level, the *KEYBOARD LAB* has become an attractive alternative to individual lessons for many students and teachers.

Teachers enjoy increased revenue and a decrease in the number of hours they teach. Students enjoy the versatility of the lab, the opportunity to be creative, and the lack of pressure that usually attends the weekly individual lesson.

In my opinion, the keyboard lab is a useful alternative to the traditional individual lesson, but student outcomes are significantly different as compared to individual study. That weekly individual lesson with its attendant need to practice and prepare a mini-concert for a teacher is an effective way to learn the piano. It is also an expensive and often wasteful way to learn to play the piano. If the student is not highly motivated or if the practice is not well done, the student does not make the progress expected, and the individual attention and focus is largely wasted.

The group lesson gives the student the advantage of semi-anonymity. He or she is not obliged to play that weekly mini-recital and can learn and be reinforced by others doing the same kind of work.

But playing the piano is fundamentally a solo activity. Unlike band, orchestra, or choir, the pianist is on her or his own. That spotlight is on her or him, even if the piano's role is that of accompanist. The only real way to learn to play the piano is to play the piano. Alone! The longer the student can avoid playing alone, the less likely their progress will lead them to playing sufficiency.

For piano students in the nineteenth and twentieth centuries, the *MASTER CLASS* was and still is viewed as a species of group lesson. A group of accomplished or apprentice pianists gather, the master teacher listens, and each member of the group takes a turn playing for the others. Usually everyone—colleagues and teacher—offers comments. But generally, these classes are supplemented by individual lessons at another time. So this *MASTER CLASS* is a kind of mid-point between lessons and concert hall, a time and place to try oneself and compare notes. This is quite a different circumstance from today's group piano lesson where individual playing is minimal or nonexistent. Ensemble playing certainly is a valuable experience, especially for beginning or less experienced students, but it is not a substitute for solo playing.

It is both the challenge and the satisfaction of piano study that in its most fundamental sense, playing the piano is an individual enterprise. Lessons suggest what to do and how to do it, but you play as well as you practice. It is not a team sport and you are beholden to no other player besides the tuner. Your success is your own and your goals are the ones you set for yourself.

Piano lessons are one of the last refuges of rugged individualism in our culture.

Chapter Twelve

Memorizing

It has become traditional for solo pianists to *MEMORIZE* their music. By "memorize," musicians would usually mean "playing without the score," a relatively new tradition that probably owes its popularity to Franz Liszt. That consummate showman is credited with being the first public pianist to play his solo recitals with his profile to the audience and a noticeable absence of a score on the instrument. To this day, non-pianists find it little short of miraculous that a mere mortal can remember all those notes without looking at a page. And indeed, while it is not a miracle, playing without a visible score—playing from memory—does require extensive preparation, analysis, and confidence.

The advantages of playing a solo piano piece without having to look at the score are obvious. A piano piece has a lot of notes, spread throughout both hands and usually obliging attention to the *RIGHT (DAMPER)* and often the *LEFT (UNA CORDA) PEDALS*. A difficult piano piece can include literally dozens and even hundreds of notes to be played in a fairly short period of time.

The geography of the piano keyboard covers eighty-eight keys. These eighty-eight keys measure forty eight inches—four feet—from the bass notes of the keyboard to the top treble note, and six inches from the front of the keys to the fallboard.

That's a lot of distance for two hands and ten fingers to cover when you're looking upward at the music rack!

Everyone needs to look at the keyboard from time to time. But every time a pianist sneaks a glance at the keyboard, she or he risks the possibility of losing her or his place on the printed page. All pianists learn to play to some extent by "feel." The keyboard geography includes black keys raised above the white like small mountains on the flat landscape of the plains. Those raised black keys, arranged for the most part in groups of two and three, help the pianist orient her or his fingers to the keyboard and help the experienced pianist to play by "feel." Indeed, one of the important issues for the beginning pianist is to learn to watch the music, rather than continuously glance at the keyboard to become oriented. The less one looks at hands on the keyboard, the more comfortable one can become when playing with a score that requires attentiveness.

But having the score committed to "memory" is a big advantage when it comes to playing the piano. It allows the pianist to focus attention on the keyboard without the constant mediation of the eye and its watchfulness.

Making music on the piano is about ordering sounds. The ear—that part of the brain that processes sonorous information—needs to be in charge. The ear helps us shape the dynamic, tells us when to go slower or faster, helps us respond to the different acoustical characteristics of the piano and room, and makes us be attentive to the needs of the listeners.

For musicians, the eye and ear offer differing input sources to the brain. The information they send goes to different parts of the brain for processing. Too much reliance on the eye—reading from the score—interferes with the ear and its attentiveness, and we can easily become more of a reflexive performance machine than the shaper of an aesthetic performance.

The eye can be a distraction for pianists. The focus of the eye on the score invariably makes it more difficult or even impossible for the ear to do its job. The problem is greater because the music rack on pianos obliges the pianist to look up to see the score, and back down to see the keyboard. This visual input is different for other instruments where the musician has a more immediate tactile connection to her or his instrument and significantly smaller physical distances to cover.

You don't need to look at the violin's finger-board to find a note, or at the trumpet's keys to feel where they are. Performers on these instruments are much more able to give most of their attention to the printed page without losing their physical connection with the instrument. While these musicians also need to "hear" what they are playing as well as become "fluent" with the printed page, the contrast between eye and ear is a different challenge than that facing the pianist.

It is not unusual for an instrumentalist—a string or wind player—to be able to read and play an unfamiliar score at sight almost as well as they might after extended practice. The geography of their instrument allows them to become secure with the tactile feel of their instrument while they devote most of their attention to pattern recognition of the printed page.

A performance of a piano piece (or any piece of music!) should be more like a conversation with a friend than a rehearsed speech given to a captive audience. A conversation flows spontaneously, ideas succeed each other comfortably. There is a natural flow and give-and-take to a personal conversation that the successful piano performance tries to emulate. A score performed from memory is more likely to achieve this natural flow than a score in which the eye needs to be actively involved processing the information of the printed page.

In my opinion, "memory" does not necessarily mean "no score on the rack." One of the most astounding and convincing performances I've heard in recent years involved a famous pianist playing a Mozart concerto with orchestra. The concerto was one of the most popular in the Mozart repertoire, and the pianist had probably known this concerto since childhood and played it many times during his career. Nevertheless, the pianist chose to have the score open on the music rack, and often turned pages during orchestral interludes when he was not playing. This pianist was playing from "memory" but the score was open as a psychological prop and occasional reminder of some of the details of a twenty-five minute work.

The presence of the score did not distract from the performance. Indeed, it probably helped. Many of us are insecure about playing from memory in public performances, or simply don't have the kind of brain wiring that allows us to comfortably memorize a long, complicated piano work. Some of us are even uncomfortable with remembering a short, simple piano work. This doesn't mean that we can't learn to play the work. It simply means that putting away the score adds a dimension of discomfort that detracts from the performance.

For me, memorization has come to mean sufficient familiarity with the score that allows for a fluent, flexible performance. It doesn't mean always playing without the score. It means that when using the score, I am not going to have my eyes occupied with reading, but use the score for an occasional reference, reminder, or security blanket. My focus will be on the music that is committed to my memory in sufficient detail that I always know what notes, fingering, pedal, or dynamic changes are coming next.

In my opinion, a live piano performance is like a tape recording stored in the mind. The performance is the unrolling tape, note following note and measure following measure. At any point in the performance, the rest of the performance, both before and after, is still there, waiting to emerge as the "tape" is transferred from our mind through our arms, hands and piano until it emerges as sound.

Memory, then, is not an all or nothing situation. It includes "familiarity," "fluency," "confidence," and, most importantly, "idea" or *SOUND IMAGE*. Some pianist's speak of "photographic" memory, the ability to remember the appearance of the page and "read" the image of the page that is in their mind.

I don't dispute this claim. Our minds are capable of extraordinary tricks, and this kind of memorization is mentioned too often by reputable sources to be simply fabrication.

Similarly, all of us are familiar with "muscle memory", the memory of rote learning. A task repeated a sufficient number of times becomes habit and can be performed with no conscious thought required. Indeed, awareness during such reflexive tasks sometimes confuses the performance. Learning to use the clutch in a standard-transmission automobile and playing a difficult technical passage in Liszt have a great deal in common. They require repetitions sufficient to establish a habit of correct performance, and woe to either automobile driver or virtuoso pianist who lets consciousness interfere too much in either of these rote-acquired tasks.

Music also seems to activate the same kinds of memory which allow us to learn and remember new languages. All children unconsciously acquire language early in life, and those fortunate children who study the piano from an early age similarly learn to "hear" and "remember" the music almost without awareness. They remember pitch inflection, rhythm, and the other characteristics of the music they hear, an unconscious act, rather than a cognitive behavior. Many young persons, for example, have an almost mystical ability to accurately remember large numbers of popular song texts that older listeners find almost interchangeable. In our modern world where music is a pervasive influence, children are acquiring these memory skills almost from birth.

A pianist's musical memory, then, is a product of a number of factors: muscle memory, analysis and cognitive memory, and pitch and rhythm memory. Any one of these by itself can be effective in acquiring fluency in playing a piece on the piano. Together, they allow pianists to play ever more complicated music with more authority, fluency, and suasion.

Chapter Thirteen

Music Reading

When I was a graduate student many years ago, I had several classes in orchestration and composition with a somewhat famous professor who was an excellent pianist. His ability to read an unfamiliar orchestra score was little short of miraculous. He could sit down with an almost indecipherable manuscript of a new orchestral composition, usually of twenty-six or more staves, and proceed to play the score at the piano at sight, always in a manner that represented the musical ideas with clarity and understanding. He also usually managed to play most of the notes.

I still remember these performances with awe and wonder. When we say that a pianist can "read the fly specks on the wall," I often think of this professor, although over the years I have encountered similar feats of score reading skill in others.

Music is ordered around patterns of pitch and rhythm called *MELODY, HARMONY, TEXTURE,* and similar concepts found in the vocabulary of *MUSIC THEORY.* For the pianist, music reading involves the recognition of these patterns and the consequent muscle response. Trained musicians look for these patterns in an unfamiliar score. Some are able to recognize and react to them almost instantaneously. Others take much longer. In conversation and interview, some great pianists speak openly of their ability to *SIGHT-READ*; others feel deficient about their reading skills. In my opinion, I don't think there is any real correlation between skill and success as a pianist and the ability to read an unfamiliar score at sight.

Certainly, a high level of pianistic skill and training improves sight-reading, but I believe that score reading is a different order of thinking from learning and performing a score. The good reader sees patterns, makes instantaneous judgments about leaving out some notes and rearranging others, and often "improvises" the ideas of the music without becoming bogged down in the details of note accuracy. Indeed, some of the least successful readers are pianists who are meticulous about playing everything "correctly" and "accurately." Note accuracy and performance polish are often counterproductive to fluent sight reading.

Good sight-readers start early and read a lot of music. Music reading improves with the practice of reading, the frequent experience of plowing through unfamiliar scores nearly at tempo. The reader learns to look for the essence of the musical idea, to leave out what is not essential, to maintain a tempo and to create an idea, even if the details are not perfect. Sight reading practice is different from performance practice. There are different goals. Sight-reading strives for continuity, clarity of expression, sketching in the ideas. Performance asks for note and rhythm accuracy, thoughtfulness, contemplation: all qualities which are not possible as notes and pages go flying past in those first impressions while reading at sight for the first or second time.

Pianists today are generally not taught sight-reading as a skill to the same extent as other musicians. Instrumentalists and singers are expected to develop excellent sight reading skills as part of their professional training, but because of the very geography of the keyboard, I believe sight-reading skills are often ignored in favor of skills that can be more easily practiced and perfected.

I have always been blessed with good sight reading skills, but I remember with horror a series of piano literature classes in graduate school in which I was expected to prepare between twenty and fifty pages of piano music weekly for the class. Of course, this was in addition to my other piano assignments. My reading, or at least my faking skills, improved appreciably in short order.

Woe be the accompanist or church musician who does not, at least through experience, develop sight-reading facility. Music reading at the piano is a skill that is highly rewarded. Conversely, poor readers have far fewer opportunities as collaborative pianists.

There are a few tactics that a pianist can employ to improve their sight-reading. A metronome is essential, as is a variety of music scores and styles. It's also a good idea to choose sight-reading music somewhat easier than your level of performance.

Set the metronome at about eighty percent of the desired tempo, and play through a page at a time. Before beginning, look over the page, observing changes of key or meter signature, measures with many notes or large jumps, and similar potential trouble spots. Than play with the metronome, leaving out what needs be left out.

After the first time through the music, look back over the troublesome spots, and spend a few minutes working out the fingering, rhythm or whatever the problem, and immediately play through the excerpt again.

Repeat this process at least four times, each time trying to supply more detail and trying to be a little more accurate. Repeat the same music for at least three consecutive days. By the end of the third day, you should begin to have achieved some degree of fluency with what you are playing.

As with any piece of unfamiliar music, look at key, chord and chord progression, key change, meter and rhythmic pattern—all those analytical observations that you would normally bring to any piece of music. Just try to bring them to bear the first or second time through the music.

One of the important side effects of being a good reader is that good readers tend to learn music more quickly than poor readers. Again, this is because good music readers, whether intuitively or because of strong music concepts and vocabulary, understand how music is organized and make that understanding a part of their reading.

Music reading, in a sense, is a conditioned skill of eye and hand. But it is a conditioned skill of awareness as well as motor habit, and the more awareness, the easier the reading.

One of the great gifts teachers can bestow on their young or less experienced students is the gift of music reading. Rather than work on a few pieces of music for weeks on end, try to encourage your students to read as much music as they can. Make the distinction between "reading" and "learning" music, and encourage the "reading" as much as the "learning." Music reading is the same as language reading: the more you do, the better you get.

And what better way is there to learn the breadth and beauty of the piano literature than reading through it, however haltingly?

Chapter Fourteen

Musical Structure

All music begins and ends. Within the time covered between beginning and end are a number of other beginnings and endings, smaller units within the larger one. Some of the musical units that occur later in the proceedings are similar or the same as earlier units. Sometimes, all the units are different. Sometimes the listener is aware of the similarity or repetition of units but sometimes they are obscure or obscured and the music seems to be continuously evolving. This organization of a piece of music into units with beginnings and endings is called *MUSICAL STRUCTURE.*

A piece of music can be compared to a book that is subdivided into chapters, paragraphs, and finally sentences and clauses. A special vocabulary describes its organization and the ways in which sectioning is created. Words such as *CADENCE* and *PHRASE, TERNARY FORM* and *RONDO* describe some of these conventions of musical organization and structure.

The study of this vocabulary and its various examples is the province of *MUSIC THEORY* which in reality is anything but theoretical. The vocabulary and concepts learned in *MUSIC THEORY* are invaluable to keyboard players who need to be able to break down long, complicated pieces of piano music into smaller, more manageable and comprehensible units. A piano composition of 300 measures seems long and complicated. A 300 measure composition that is actually 30 units of about 10 measures each is much more manageable, especially when the pianist begins to recognize that 20 of the 30 units are the same or similar.

But an understanding of *MUSICAL STRUCTURE* is more than a learning aid for the pianist. In my opinion, the task of the pianist is to play the "structure" of the music, making the beginnings, endings, and evolution of ideas clear to a listener.

Pianists—indeed, all musicians—read *STRUCTURAL ORGANIZATION* in different ways. There is no "correct" reading of the organization of any piece of music. Rather, there are conventions of organization which pianists seek out and try to express. But it is not always clear where a phrase ends, or how a motive is developed. The most interesting performances are those in which the pianist "reads" the musical structure in a slightly different or unconventional way, creating an interpretation that might be new and revealing or simply idiosyncratic and confusing. An understanding and reading of *MUSICAL STRUCTURE* is fundamental to the art of interpreting any piece of music, whatever the vocabulary used to describe the ways in which the music is organized.

A rose by any other name is still a rose.

Chapter Fifteen

Notation

MUSIC NOTATION is a series of visual codes that represent pitch, time and time relationships, and dynamics. When the codes are sonorously interpreted by a pianist or other musician, the result is music.

Pitch is a fairly precise representation of specific sounds. That is, an "A" is an "A," more or less. Its visual placement on the staff represents a specific key on the piano. Pianists have it easier than other musicians. String and Wind players not only have to know what the pitch symbol "A" means, they have to also adjust their intonation to find a specific and agreed upon "A." because variable pitch instruments can produce a variety of "A"s that sound, even to the untrained ear, distinctly different. Today, the concert pitch "A" can range from 436 vibrations per second—so called "early music" tuning, to 446 vibrations per second, preferred by some professional orchestras because of the brilliance and edgy sound it imparts to the music. That's a pretty big difference in a sound represented by the same symbol!

The piano is a fixed pitch instrument. Once it is tuned, the player cannot adjust the sound. So if your piano is tuned high or tuned low, you have no control over the sound of "A." Pianists do and don't take this for granted. Our ears are sensitive to what we perceive as out-of-tune instruments, and some of us even learn to tune the instrument. Tuning is a time consuming task involving special wrenches called *TUNING HAMMERS* and an understanding of the acoustics of setting a fundamental temperament or tuning. Many of us prefer to leave the tuning to professionals. But whatever we choose, an "A" is an "A" is an "A" until we retune the instrument.

Musical notation is a little less precise about time and time relationships. We all learn early in our study that two quarter-notes equal one half-note, and an augmentation dot increases the value of a note by half. But many of us have a differing sensitivity to the duration of a note. My own proclivity is to play speedy quarter notes, and often I play less than the full duration of these notes. Some of this is personality: by nature I am a person always in a hurry. Some of this is aesthetic. "Cheating" on the duration of a note can make a passage sound more exciting, or more serene if I "cheat" in the other direction and linger on the note.

Students try to learn to play in precise time by using the metronome. Electronic metronomes tend to be more accurate than the wind-up variety, and the new digital metronomes are usually accurate. However, no pianist will want to play precisely in time all the time. Expressiveness in music is partly the consequence of hurrying or delaying the duration of the notes or measures, and so the trick is to learn how much and when to vary the units of time in a piece of music. When your choices are appropriate, compelling, or affective, your playing is described as moving, sensitive, dramatic. When your use of time seems a mis-use, your playing is described as . . . "out-of-time."

Dynamics are an even more slippery expressive slope to climb. How loud is *LOUD*? How soft is *SOFT*? *MEDIUM-LOUD*? *FORTISSIMO*? All of us early in our study realize that these terms are relative and serve mostly as general guideposts to dynamic levels and dynamic variety. The dynamic signs in music notation—loud, soft, crescendo—are like saying *GO WEST* or *GO EAST*, generally helpful but only to a point.

Similarly, tempo indications such as *FAST* or *MODERATELY* are so vague as to offer great latitude to the reader of the score. Performance conventions are probably as important in this regard as the actual written directions. Few pianists would play the opening bars of Beethoven's *MOONLIGHT SONATA* at a fast tempo and loud dynamic. It would simply be beyond the performance conventions that have been established over a period of almost two hundred years. But performance conventions are a different issue than reading the tempo and dynamic directions as they are marked on the page.

All this is to suggest that *NOTATION* in music is at best a series of vague directions, more specific than *BLUES IN E FLAT*, but significantly less precise than $3X=12$. Actually, like an algebraic formula, we need to know the values before we can solve the musical equation. Unlike the algebraic formula, however, each pianist will solve the equation in a slightly different manner because the values are personal, not quantifiable.

The interpretation of *MUSIC NOTATION* is an art, not science.

Chapter Sixteen

Pedal

Discussions of *PEDAL* in the literature of pianists and piano playing seem to arouse the most heated exchanges and opinions. If pianists sometimes seem theological in their beliefs, then the *PEDAL* must be the pianist's *ORIGINAL SIN!*

There are three pedals on most acoustic pianos, upright and grand, and it is the *RIGHT* or *DAMPER* pedal that generates the most controversy. The *LEFT* pedal, called *UNA CORDA,* does what its name implies: it shifts the keyboard so that the hammers strike only one or two strings. Normally, the hammers of a grand piano will strike all three strings (or one or two in the lower part of the instrument), so this shifting of the keyboard means that the sound immediately is "softened," and the "color" of the piano sound is changed. A similar effect is attained in upright pianos by shortening the distance of the hammer stroke. Indeed, the left pedal is sometimes called the "soft" pedal, and its most usual purpose is to achieve a quiet, hushed quality of sound.

Even today, many pianists believe that it is "cheating" to use the left pedal to create that softer dynamic. There is not much question that a soft dynamic achieved without the left pedal is different from the soft sound achieved with the left pedal. So what? There is no absolute meaning to the concept of "soft" in piano playing. "Soft" takes its meaning in contrast to "loud" and the "soft" pedal adds another option to the pianist's arsenal of expressive possibilities. Many pianists will never have the technical skill to command a variety of tonal dynamics, and the soft pedal is an easy way to create more dynamic variety in one's playing. Why not use all the expressive possibilities at one's command?

The *MIDDLE* pedal—*TRE CORDA*—is a special effects pedal, selectively sustaining lower notes on the piano. When this pedal is depressed correctly, the *DAMPER* or *RIGHT* pedal can be used in the usual manner, so the *TRE*

CORDA pedal creates an effect something like a limited organ pedal. There are very few occasions when the middle pedal can be used, and they are mostly the province of highly skilled professionals. I normally would suggest a kind of benign neglect.

The *RIGHT* or *DAMPER* pedal, is the device that occasions so much pianistic controversy. Sometimes the right pedal is called the *LOUD* pedal, in contrast to the left or *SOFT* pedal. When the damper pedal is depressed by the right foot, the dampers that rest on the strings inside the piano all are raised, and all the strings in the piano vibrate freely. Contrast this sound with the sound of one damper raised above one set of strings. (Each pitch on the piano has one, two or three strings, depending upon the style of the piano and its manufacturer.) The strings of the piano cannot vibrate when the *DAMPERS* are resting upon them. The *DAMPERS*, made of felt topped with wood, rest upon the strings and keep them from vibrating. When the dampers rest on the strings, no sound can be produced.

When a pianist strikes a single key, several things happen. The key activates the hammer to rise up and strike the string (from underneath on a grand piano or from the front on an upright piano), but striking the key also lifts the damper from that string. Thus the hammer striking the string causes the string to vibrate freely and creates the sound of that pitch. If the damper remained on the string, there would be little or no sound because the string could not vibrate.

You can sample this effect for yourself. In almost all pianos, the top two octaves have no dampers. Place your finger on one of these damper-less strings and play the note. You get a "thud", but no resonating sound. The string can't vibrate with your finger on it.

When the damper is off the string(s), the string(s) are free to vibrate. When the damper falls back on the string, the sound is "damped" and stops. If the damper never fell back to the string, the sound would still die away, because friction with the air stops the vibration of the string in a fairly short time. Thus, the sound produced by a vibrating piano string either decays slowly, or the damper stops the sound completely.

There is no way to sustain a sound on an acoustic piano beyond a short interval of time. Contrast this, for example, with a synthesizer whose sound is produced electronically and can be sustained indefinitely if desired. String players can also sustain a sound by changing the direction of the bow and wind players have developed a method of "circular" breathing that similarly allows an almost continuous stream of air to sustain a sound for a long period of time.

This cannot be done on the acoustic piano. The length of a sound is limited by the acoustics of the instrument. Figurations such as *TREMOLO, REPEATED NOTE,* and *ALBERTI BASS* are some of the tactics that composers have devised to sustain a sound or gesture on an instrument that is basically non-sustaining. Remember that the piano is a *Percussion* instrument!

When the key is released, the damper falls back to the string and the sound stops. This has been an ongoing problem for pianists, who have eighty-eight keys and only ten fingers. Further, one of the basic characteristics of music in our culture is *LEGATO*—the sense that sounds connect to one another and often overlap. "Sustainability" is one of the most important qualities in our music. Thus, one of the fundamental issues facing the pianist is how to quickly change registers but still sustain the sound, especially when the next sound is not within the convenient span of the hand?

Enter the "damper" pedal. As every pianist quickly learns, the damper pedal allows a sound to be sustained when the hand is lifted from the key. The sound is sustained because the damper can't fall back to stop the string as long as the pedal is depressed. The sound will still decay but more slowly.

Any pitch produced when the damper pedal is depressed sounds different than the same pitch produced without the damper pedal. In addition to sustaining the sound, the damper pedal *COLORS* the sound with the freely resonating *OVERTONES* of all those other strings that vibrate because their dampers also are raised above the strings.

A simple experiment will demonstrate the *COLOR* of these resonating overtones. Depress the damper pedal and whistle or shout into the open piano. A variety of sounds will answer you. The damper pedal is not selective. It lifts ALL the dampers off ALL the strings, and allows all the strings to freely resonate and mingle with each other.

OVERTONES are an acoustical phenomenon. When any fundamental sound is made, a number of sounds above the fundamental—some audible, some almost unheard—will freely resonate. It is this free resonance of *OVERTONES* that *COLORS* the sound of the piano when the damper pedal is used.

One can then summarize the uses of the damper pedal as follows:

> The damper pedal sustains sounds. This allows the pianist to play legato throughout the four foot geography of the piano keyboard.
>
> The damper pedal "colors" sounds by allowing for the free resonance and mingling of all the strings of the piano, not just the few activated by individual keys.

The sound of the modern acoustic piano with the resonance created by the damper pedal is akin to the vibrato we associate with a string instrument or voice. With our ears conditioned by all manner of modern listening experiences, we have come to expect the characteristic sound of the modern acoustic piano to be that which includes the damper pedal.

And here lies the root of the pedal controversy among pianists. Some like it rich and resonating, some like it dry and crisp. Modern recordings like it dry and crisp because the sound is easier to record and engineer. Audiences like it rich and resonating, especially in large, multi-purpose halls which are often acoustically engineered for little or no reverberation. We like to be engulfed by our music, not mildly tickled.

The piano as an instrument is meant to imitate the human voice without the limitations of the voice. To create that illusion of "singing tone"—the perfect legato—which is the ideal of most pianists, the damper pedal must play a significant role. Not coincidentally, the piano as an evolving technology reached the high point of its expressive popularity about the same time as the problems of the pedal apparatus and the acoustical resonance of the mechanism were resolved. "Singing – tone" and "orchestral resonance" as we understand them today are possible only because of the damper pedal.

Why, then, the reluctance on the part of many pianists to embrace the damper pedal and all it can do for piano music. Aesthetic preferences certainly vary, but most engineers would not argue that the abacus is more efficient than the computer in doing their work. Yet many pianists and piano instructors are particularly wary of the damper pedal, teach its use badly when they teach it at all, and in their own playing eschew it whenever possible. I cannot count the number of times I've heard students relate that they were told to keep both feet flat on the floor for the first several years of study. But then, there are still teachers who teach piano playing one hand at a time. Unlike bad engineering, bad piano teaching is usually held unaccountable.

I sometimes feel that pianists who use little or no damper pedal are more interested in their own virtuosity than communicating with their audiences, and indeed, audiences while frequently astonished by this digital clarity and dexterity, often are psychologically and emotionally less than fully satisfied. While audience response and virtuoso motivation are not really the issue in this discussion, the question of what is "too much pedal" is still very much a heated discussion amongst pianists and teachers.

The damper pedal used too abundantly creates a mishmash of sounds that makes it hard to follow the melodic line and blurs ideas in a confusion of undifferentiated sound. Sometimes this kind of performance can be oddly appealing, even as it seems inappropriate. But I believe that too much pedal is the consequence of confusion about what the pedal can and should do.

One of the basic misunderstandings about the damper pedal arises from the piano's role as both a harmonic and melodic instrument. Because the piano can play many sounds simultaneously—harmony—it is often thought of as a "harmonic" instrument, and it accomplishes this role admirably. However, changing the damper pedal according to harmonic changes is a misunderstanding of the instrument and of our perceptual preferences for most music, and, in my opinion, is a misuse of the damper pedal.

The piano is fundamentally a "melodic" instrument. It can play many melodies simultaneously—harmony—but it can also define a melody as clearly and as beautifully as any single line instrument or voice that performs only one melody at a time.

If we think of the damper pedal as a device that helps us define the principal melody—the "narrative"—of the music, we will never misuse the damper pedal. The first task in playing a piano piece is to find, define, and present the narrative melody of the piece, however obscure or disjointed it might be. Music is fundamentally about narrative, and the challenge to any performer is to understand and present this narrative in a convincing manner. The damper pedal helps us define the narrative and create the connections—the legato—between the sounds of the narrative. The damper pedal also creates the most vibrant "colors" for those sounds through the free mingling of all those overtones.

Artur Rubinstein once told me (and many others on other occasions): "The damper pedal is the soul of the piano."

I believe there are two fundamental and different ways to use the damper pedal. For want of a standard terminology, I describe these as *LEGATO* or *SUSTAINING* pedal; and *COLOR* pedal.

LEGATO or *SUSTAINING* pedal is also known as "syncopated" pedaling in the pedagogical literature and is the most frequently discussed style of pedaling. Basically, the foot begins in a down position, the pedal depressed. As the piano key is played by the finger, the pedal is raised and again immediately depressed so the sound is sustained. The key goes down, the pedal goes up and down. Once the pedal is back down, the sound will sustain, whether the finger remains on the key or goes to the next key. It is important to recognize that the sound of the pedaled note cannot be altered once it is achieved, so it is not only logical but ergonomically efficient to move the finger to the next note, allowing the pedal to sustain the note already played.

COLOR pedal is exactly the opposite of legato pedaling and aims only to create the "color" of the overtones without running sounds together. With "color" pedal, the foot begins from an "up" position, depresses the pedal for a short time, and clears (returns to the up position) as appropriate. The "color" of the overtones is added but the legato or blur is not. "Color" pedal requires careful attention as well as a complete lift of the damper pedal. "Lift" means that the dampers clear the string but need to be allowed to return to completely cut off all string vibration.

Finally, a small discussion of pedal markings in printed music is in order. Frequently, no pedal or infrequent pedaling is marked in a score. Sometimes, the pedal marking, particularly in editions done by 19th century editors, seems idiosyncratic if not downright inappropriate. As with all markings on the printed page, the pedal marks need be interpreted, not only in the context of modern instruments, but in the context of the pianist's particular sound image. I am never sure that composers, even the great pianist composers, were able to completely convey their sonorous images via the printed page. But I have come to believe that whatever their original intention, it is up to the individual pianist to create an image that reflects, not only the printed page, but also the best considered musical judgment of the player. In this sense, the pianist must be "creator" as well as "re-creator", and nowhere is this more important and telling than in the use of the damper pedal.

Chapter Seventeen

Physicality and Relaxation

The piano usually is played with two hands, two feet, and one head. 'Two heads are better than one . . . sometimes.' (Sidney Foster) A good instructor or a thoughtful listener is invaluable to pianists of all levels. It is very hard for a pianist to objectively hear what she or he is doing. A trusted set of ears—head #2—is always desirable.

Of the physical equipment needed, I have come to believe that the head has perhaps the most value. Good hands and a sensitive pedaling are essential tools, but unless the tools are given direction, they are just tools.

Relaxation is an important part of successful piano playing. Relaxation means something different to each person who thinks about it, but essentially, relaxation permits ergonomic efficiency. Ergonomic efficiency means you can do more with less effort. Some of the world's great pianists have been incredibly tense, stiff and unrelaxed. They played because of their strong concept and in spite of the tension in their arms and body. It is better to learn something about how to relax the arms, shoulders, body, and mind. *Yoga* and *Alexander Technique* are two of the often-used practices that encourage relaxation.

Relaxation basically means don't use more muscle tension than is necessary to accomplish the task. The latest buzz word to describe minimum tension is *'ergonomic efficiency,'* a term borrowed from efficiency experts who work in manufacturing and mass production. The job of efficiency experts is to find more effective ways of accomplishing a task. The ergonomic computer keyboard is one example of their work.

In piano playing, ergonomic efficiency means, for example, to use minimum muscle tension to hold the arms in place over the keyboard. To experience this, put the arms into playing position and tighten the muscles as much as you can. Than relax the muscles as much as you can without letting your arms fall off the keyboard. There is a huge difference between maximum and minimum muscle exertion in this simple exercise.

Think about your shoulders and upper body. Are they held stiff and tense in anticipation of the difficult work to come? Breathe a few times and try to drop the shoulders and relax the upper body and arm muscles as much as possible. Ergonomic efficiency. Minimum muscle tension. Maximum muscle relaxation between exertions.

All athletes know how to relax in the moments between the maximum exertions frequently demanded by their sport. Why should pianists not learn this simple athletic truth?

The four fingers that are not the thumb are used more efficiently when they are rounded and played on the tip. The first joint below these fingertips is similarly more effective when kept rounder. The thumb (and often the fifth finger) usually is played on the side between the tip and first joint, and most often played in conjunction with dropping the wrist.

All of these notions are true and untrue. Piano technique—physicality at the piano—is an enormously complicated subject and best explained by a competent teacher. Indeed, it always seems to me that this is mostly what a piano teacher should do. Any sensitive listener can coach: *a little louder in measure 4, crescendo in measure 8, subito piano in the next measure and play the left hand softer. Technic*—how to physically play the instrument in a comfortable and effective manner—is far more complicated and is usually ignored by most teachers, either because they are uncomfortable with the work, or more likely, because they are unfamiliar with developing effective physicality at the piano. It is far easier to tell a student to play the same passage 200 times at a slow tempo than to suggest how the hand and arm might adapt themselves to the complex movements required to effectively negotiate the passage.

Physicality at the piano can and should be taught. A large body of literature has been devoted to the subject, and a competent teacher should have both a point of view about piano technique and familiarity with the literature that represents many points of view. There is no "correct" way to play the piano, except the way that works for the player. There are useful concepts of relaxation, hand and arm position, and physicality which are effective and students should not have to reinvent the wheel as they learn to play. If a teacher is unable or unwilling to help a student with piano technique—physicality and relaxation—the student should find another teacher.

All musicality is the consequence of physicality applied to creating a musical concept. At the piano, musical ideas without the necessary physical resources to accomplish the task are difficult if not impossible, and limited physical resources invariably lead to frustration and eventually, defeat. Many students simply give up because they are not able to realize their musical ideas, and have no idea about how to resolve this impasse. The common criticism to an unsuccessful student is 'No Talent,' but more often than not, the real criticism is 'Bad teaching.'

Chapter Eighteen

Piano

STEINWAY. YAMAHA. BALDWIN. BOSENDOERFER. PLEYEL. YOUNG CHANG. KAWAI. KORG. ACROSONIC. STORY AND CLARK. KIMBALL.

The list of piano manufacturers runs to dozens and perhaps hundreds of names. Some of them no longer manufacture pianos although a valued relic from the past will often turn up at a garage sale or auction.

Many years ago, I read in the classifieds about a seven foot Bechstein grand piano available for six hundred dollars at a garage sale. My wife's family was in need of an instrument to replace their old upright piano that was no longer fixable.

Any piano can be "gutted"—its insides replaced, its exterior refinished—and made like new if one is willing to pay the price. Indeed, there is an upscale market for very expensive antique pianos that are in excellent playing shape. They grace many a luxury home's living room in a place of honor.

Bechstein is one of the legendary names in pianos. A new instrument of that size at the time would have cost more than a luxury automobile. I quickly drove to the sale, looked at a beautiful wooden case in excellent condition, and played a piano with obvious mechanical problems that still managed to perform with some degree of elegance. Sold.

The weight of the piano was significant, and the cost of moving the instrument across town added significantly to the initial price. Closer inspection by an expert technician revealed an instrument in need of extensive repairs including a new pin block and new sound board. We chose to leave the instrument mostly as it was with a few essential patch-ups so that all the notes sounded. It was to serve as a practice piano for my wife and me when we were in town, and as a home instrument for my wife's mother who was a talented but not very experienced pianist. It served these purposes admirably for many years although it frequently needed tuning and mechanical repairs to keep it in minimal playing condition. We gave it away when my wife's parents moved. I'm still not sure it would not have been just as good an idea to redo the insides of the piano and put it in good playing condition. This would have cost many thousands of dollars but would still have cost much less than a new instrument of comparable quality. There was something elegant about that piano, as often there is about old and beat-up instruments that have seen better days. If only these instruments could tell their stories, we would be amazed.

I am often asked to evaluate used pianos by students or friends. I always suggest that they play the instrument and see if they like its personality and feel. If they do, I suggest they pay a qualified technician to go over the instrument and see what kinds of repairs, minor and major, might be required to keep the piano playing. In my opinion, a person should never buy an instrument unless they feel some affinity for it, whether the connection is the piano's physical appearance, its tone and overall sound, or the way it plays. Pianos have personalities, and your personality must mesh with the instrument to have a comfortable fit.

Remember when buying any piano, new or old, that the room and its furnishings affect how the piano sounds, and thus, how it feels to play. A room that is acoustically dead will often detract from the "feel" of a piano that would be perfectly lovely in a room with more acoustic ambiance. Similarly, many piano showrooms are acoustically "live," and a piano that goes into your living room with its curtains, rugs and furniture, may well sound and feel very different than the instrument you played on and bought from the showroom floor.

New pianos range in cost from expensive to really expensive. A small acoustic grand piano today can easily cost $15,000 for a less expensive brand, and the Steinway and Yamaha models often cost $40,000 and more. Upright and console pianos are always less costly than grand pianos and are easier to fit into a smaller living space.

A few words about synthesizers. These instruments are actually small computers whose sounds are produced or reproduced technologically. Almost all these instruments today are touch sensitive and come with pedal attachments. On one occasion, I played a classical piano recital on one of these keyboards, as it was far superior to the acoustic relic that graced the concert hall. Aside from the appearance, the audience seemed quite satisfied with the result.

Synthesizers are often given a traditional wing-shaped grand piano case, although the case is strictly for appearance and the sound and amplification are produced technologically. These instruments can create all manner of special effects and can sound like, among others, a Steinway Piano in Carnegie Hall or in Boston's Symphony Hall. These are the wonders of synthesized, or in this case, sampled sounds. Electronic instruments do not go out of tune and can be played with headphones so that there is no intrusive sound for apartment dwellers. There are many advantages to these electronic pianos and they should not be dismissed out of hand. Perhaps most importantly, they are significantly less expensive than their acoustic predecessors, a fact that often makes the difference when one is seeking a keyboard instrument for personal use.

Whatever the choice of "Piano"—acoustic, electronic, new, old—the keyboard functions in the same way. It is an input device through which the player creates sounds and combinations of sounds. Whatever the instrument, its size, and its cost, the potential of the "Piano" to enchant and amaze still seems limitless.

Chapter Nineteen

Posture

Franz Liszt, consummate musician and showman, is said to have begun the practice of turning the piano sideways to the audience, both for acoustic clarity, and at least partially so that his magnificent profile would command attention as he played.

Whether or not there is merit in this old story, there is no question that pianists often are aware of the "theatrics" of performance, and their body language—posture—and facial gestures frequently reflect almost as much rehearsal as the actual playing of the notes. With music videos becoming an important medium for performance today, body language and posture is increasingly one of the issues that pianists address.

Unhappily, that which looks good is not always helpful to the performer. Posture at the keyboard should above all emphasize comfort and ergonomic efficiency. The idea still is the playing of the notes to communicate a musical story, and awkward posture, facial grimaces, and elaborate hand gestures can get in the way of a performance, however much they might help sell tickets.

It was well known that the great Artur Rubinstein, when launching into Manuel de Falla's *RITUAL FIRE DANCE,* a work he often played as an encore, would fling his arms high above the keyboard in a display of physical bravura visible at the back of the hall. Unhappily, I once heard him miss many of the opening notes because of his gestures. But I'm sure in Rubinstein's mind the theatre of the moment was worth the risk of some wrong notes.

We normally try to sit comfortably in the middle of the keyboard, with our body slightly to the right of middle C, since the right hand plays more often toward the extremes of the right side of the keyboard. The height of the body can usually be adjusted by raising or lowering an adjustable artist's bench. If an adjustable bench is not available, it is important to sit at a height in which the elbows can hang freely. It is preferable to sit lower than higher. Indeed, I know of one virtuoso who claimed his ultimate goal was to sit at the piano using only the Manhattan Telephone Directory as a bench.

The upper body and shoulders should be as relaxed as possible. Pianists often scrunch up their shoulders which can create a backache or sore hand. Try to let the shoulders drop, and the arms hang freely.

To bob and weave or to remain stationary while playing? I think the player should do what seems natural and comfortable, although too much body movement can create visual distractions for a listener, and become tiring to the player. Whichever choice, it is still important to try and avoid unnecessary tension in the body, shoulders, or arms.

With the advent of inexpensive video cameras, many piano teachers film their students with the idea that one picture is worth a thousand words. It is useful for a student to see herself or himself while playing. Often, the pianist is unaware of her or his posture, and watching a video can show far more clearly than many words of explanation. Still, the pianist needs to find a comfort zone at the instrument.

Playing the piano for long periods of time can become an uncomfortable physical experience, and it is useful to get up frequently to move about and stretch the muscles. No matter how relaxed and comfortable the posture, all pianists get physically fatigued from sitting in front of the instrument and practicing, often for hours at a time. Muscle ache, tension, and sometimes physical damage can occur. One of my instructors was a world famous pianist who spent many years in a special back brace, the consequence of too much practice in too rigid a position.

After studying the fundamentals of good piano technique, relaxation, and perhaps yoga, the best advice one can give any pianist is to "Listen to your body." If it hurts, stop. If it gets stiff or sore, move about and stretch. Piano playing is a physical endeavor. We are athletes as well as artists and need to pay attention to our posture as well as our art.

Chapter Twenty

Practicing

"How do I get to Carnegie Hall?" asks the tourist, emerging from the 57th Street subway stop.

"Practice!"

The following are a few quotations from PIANISTS ON PLAYING: INTERVIEWS WITH TWELVE CONCERT PIANISTS. Linda J. Noyle. The Scarecrow Press, Inc. Metuchen, N. J. & London. 1987

> Practice is a very personal matter. I don't really like practicing per se! I practice at the piano only when I feel it is required—and no more than an hour and a half at any one time. I believe I am the only person who can decide how much practice is useful and productive.
> *Jorge Bolet* (page 14)

> First of all, every artist gets angry in practicing. He gets angry at the music, or he gets angry at himself for his own stupidity. So there are times that you hit the keyboard, and there are times you swear four-letter language. It's hard work. It's like dishwashing. It isn't fun. About fifty percent of practicing is not fun.
> *John Browning* (page 26)

> The best hours for practice are the morning hours when a person's mind is fresh and the ears are fresh, and also when, hopefully, there are no telephone interruptions. I find that a one-hour period is where I achieve the utmost in terms of concentration. I work very intensively for one hour and then take a ten, fifteen, or twenty-minute break during which I will occupy myself with something completely different, whether it's to eat or something else. This method works out well so that I can continue for eight hours, in one-hour periods, if there's time enough for that. In general, the more you practice, the better. That's really true. But the best is to practice with a fresh head, a rested mind, otherwise, you're not going to be productive.
> *Bella Davidovich* (page 43)

I sit down in the morning and I finish at the end of the day, and that's it. I don't even break for a meal. Practicing can go on for nine hours easily in a stretch, without taking a break. But I'm also practicing chamber music, repertoire for recordings, and music for two pianos with my wife.
Misha Dichter (pages 53–54)

All practicing is for performance.
Janina Fialkowska (page 71)

Concentration is very tiring. It depends upon whether you are at home or not at home. It depends upon your physical state, sometimes you feel fresh, sometimes you feel tired. It gets complicated. Sometimes one or two hours of concentrated practicing is much more tiring than playing seven or eight hours. That's just the way it is.
Rudolf Firkusny (page 83)

When I was studying at the conservatory, I practiced as many hours as I physically could. I have to admit more than six or seven hours a day. People forget the hard work they put in. When you read that this one didn't practice hard, don't believe it, because you tend to forget. I know I did it, and I know that other people did it, too. There's no getting around the amount of work . . . you get to a different level of conditioning. With the piano, there's no way of getting around those hours at the piano if you practice to play correctly.
Andre-Michel Schub (page 108)

I practice not more than two hours at a time because I get tired. After that there is no concentration, so it is not worthwhile. Two hours in one sitting is maximum. The most important thing in practicing is not to waste time. Fooling yourself is the biggest crime that most music students make. Very often gifted people sometimes like to fool themselves into thinking that they are great artists . . . The idea is to get sixty minutes of value out of the sixty minutes you spend at the piano.
Abbey Simon (page 122)

Practicing, the dreaded "P" word, is the bane of students and teachers alike. It should not be. Practicing is learning, those times when the pianist develops and refines the sound ideas that will become music in performance. It is also the time when the pianist develops the fluency that allows for ease and security of communication of the ideas found in the notes. So *PRACTICING* really means *DISCOVERY, INTERPRETATION, INTROSPECTION, DEVELOPMENT OF FLUENT EXPRESSION,* and a number of other skills we don't often associate with the notion of 'time spent at the piano.'

PLANNING is one of the most important skills involved in practicing. Many students equate "practice" with "time spent." Practicing well does take a good deal of time, but the least effective kind of practicing is the rote repetition of notes for a given period of time. Two hours practice a day is no more a guarantee of success as a pianist that two hours of school homework a day, although no hours a day in either endeavor is a formula for failure. Two hours of PLANNED practice each day is a guarantee of progress, although I must add that progress in piano playing is incremental and usually occurs in spurts rather than in smooth steady development.

"Planning" means deciding what needs to be accomplished, dividing up the larger task into a number of reasonable small tasks that are doable, and organizing the small tasks into specific activities of which repetition plays an important part. Playing the piano is both an art and a sport, involving intellectual insight but also the development of highly refined small-motor skills. As with any athletic activity, the skills associated with piano playing require many repetitions until they become automatic as well as conscious. A baseball player swings the bat countless times to develop the proper control but also an automatic response. Similarly, the pianist needs to devote MANY repetitions to a variety of small tasks to assure a comfortable, almost automatic response during the performance of the larger piece of music.

A plan of practice for a week may involve a large objective, such as:

> Learn to play the first three pages of this composition fluently at metronome tempo "Quarter note = 74."

A practice plan will also include a number of small tasks such as:

> Work out and write in the fingering for measures 8–12.
> Practice the left hand in measures 18–25 ten times alone to develop fluency.
> Divide the three pages up into four and eight bar phrases.
> Practice the difficult final page ten times each day to develop security.

A plan such as this has a large general goal, but also suggests a number of small tasks that, when followed, will help achieve the larger goal.

Planning is different for each composition and for each week of practice. Since most piano lessons meet weekly, it is a good idea to work out plans in weekly as well as daily increments, although it is also helpful to set larger goals for larger units of time, such as:

Learn to play from memory three pieces during the next 15 weeks.

It is helpful to write down your plan and keep a record of what you actually accomplish. This written record will help you develop a reasonable plan based upon your actual activity.

Learning how to develop a usable practice plan is essential if you wish to make progress as a pianist without dampening or destroying your enthusiasm for music and the piano. Notice that there is nothing in this discussion that says "Practice X hours each day or week." Practicing is not an exercise in time consumption. Your plan and your commitment will tell you how many hours daily and weekly you need practice. Practice time should be dictated by objectives and musical goals, not the clock.

Practicing requires that you pay careful attention. The object of practicing is to learn to play a piece of music. This seems so obvious that it needs repeating: THE OBJECT OF PRACTICING IS TO LEARN TO PLAY A PIECE OF MUSIC. Each time you practice, you need to be attentive to how closely your playing—and practicing—comes to your musical objectives. You need to learn to hear yourself critically, to judge your work as you are doing it. Critical attention is perhaps the most important and elusive skill in intelligent practicing. I can't count the number of students who, in amazement, have told me in conversation: "You mean I have to listen to myself??!!"

Yes, each time you play you should be listening to yourself and trying to mold that recalcitrant instrument of wood, metal, and petrochemicals through the skills of your reluctant fingers and arms into the idealized sound model which your musical imagination has devised. No easy task!

Let us recognize an important psychological reaction to practicing. Practicing the piano is challenging, deeply satisfying, and often exhilarating, but practicing is hardly "fun" in the everyday sense of the word. Many pianists in their practice look for the kind of instant success that they associate with other, different activities, and are disappointed or discouraged because of unreal expectations and seemingly slow progress. Piano playing requires *TENACITY*, a willingness and insistence on working to achieve what is best in oneself, rather than accepting someone else's view of what constitutes art.

Piano playing is a humanistic endeavor. It gives us back what we put in and helps us understand and reveal some of our fundamental values. While others can show us the way and help us avoid "reinventing the wheel," we fundamentally teach ourselves. This is a worthy but difficult task not always valued in our highly complex, technological society in which teamwork and systems have largely replaced individual achievement.

Some specific objectives of practice:

1. Play the correct notes. Many piano students "fudge." All pianists will occasionally play wrong notes in a performance, but the correct notes should be learned from the beginning. This often obliges the pianist to go extremely slowly at first.
2. Play the correct rhythm. When in doubt, count it out. Subdivide. Play the correct rhythm from the first day. Also use the metronome regularly. The value of this inexpensive time-keeper/substitute teacher cannot be overstated.

3. Make pedal decisions as the sound image evolves and when necessary, write them in the score. Pedal ideas will change as the pianist becomes more familiar with the score and sound image becomes clearer. Nevertheless, make conscious pedal decisions and treat them with the same care as notes and rhythms.
4. Analyze the score from the first reading. Exhaustive analysis is not a precondition to learning and analysis evolves along with the intuitive aspect of sound image. Nevertheless, a piece of music must be understood to be played persuasively and analysis provides that understanding.
5. Follow the composer's descriptive directions. Much in music is implied or conveyed by the choice of pitch and rhythm, but composers also provide information describing, at least generally, the dynamics, tempo and psychological mood. However limited these words may be, they convey musical intent and help one in developing a personal sound image. Composer's directions should be scrupulously observed and then, on occasion, disregarded. This obliges the pianist to pay attention to what they are.
6. Play expressively from the first reading. Time and dynamics are an essential part of music. Vary them and incorporate them in your playing at all times. Always try to play expressively.
7. Remember that sight reading is different than practicing. Sight-reading means *CONTINUITY*: keep going! Practicing means *DEVELOP* or *IMPROVE*! Don't sight read when you should be practicing . . . and vice-versa!
8. When in doubt, mark all fingering and pedaling in the score.
9. Practice what you don't know. Perform what you do.
10. Practice the same pieces or units for at least three consecutive days. The second day's practice will be more fluent than the first and the third will really show signs of improvement. Follow-up practice is essential for learning and retention.
11. Practice every day. A little time spent each day is far better than a lot of time spent once or twice a week. A lot of time spent every day is better than a little time. A lot of time spent several times a day is the most effective way to stay fresh and interested and to improve retention.
12. Practice HANDS TOGETHER unless there is a specific reason to practice hands separately. Learning a piece one hand at a time is inefficient and guarantees that your sight-reading skills will never improve.
13. Practice with the metronome.
14. Practice with a cassette recorder and listen to your practice sessions occasionally. Also, perform for your cassette recorder. It will give you accurate feedback and help give you confidence for when you perform for people.

15. When possible, practice from memory at half-tempo. This is the most effective way to gain security, accuracy, and self-confidence.
16. Don't practice quickly when you should be going slowly. Don't practice slowly when you should be going quickly. Don't practice more quickly than you can play accurately when you're first learning a piece. Don't keep practicing a piece of music slowly when you know it and should be practicing how you want it to sound.

Think hard about the ideas of practicing. This is how pianists spend most of their time, and it is important for you to develop tactics that help you be successful and enjoy the music and the piano. Practicing can be hard work, but practicing should not become drudgery. You can learn to make your practicing stimulating, productive and enjoyable!

"How do I get to Carnegie Hall?" "Take the Red Line from Canarsie and transfer at 14th Street, than . . ."

Chapter Twenty-One

Repertoire

There are more pieces written for the piano than a pianist can play in many lifetimes. In addition to the enormous variety of music written originally for the instrument, there are at least as many pieces of music arranged or transcribed for it. The piano can play everything and anything, and most pieces of music eventually find their way to its music rack in one form or another.

Before the advent of radio, TV and recordings, the piano was a kind of home entertainment center. Transcriptions of the latest opera or symphony; four hand arrangements of popular songs of the day; innumerable church hymnals: if it was music, it was played on the piano. The same is true today. Any music store will stock arrangements of the latest theme music from popular TV shows or films and often, the arrangements can be had in big note, intermediate difficulty, or semi-virtuoso versions.

An enterprising pianist can also down-load a seemingly endless variety of scores from computer web sites, both legal and illicit, and the traditional classical repertoire is still largely in print and available although the less familiar works are becoming more difficult to find. Copyright laws are quite clear about what is legal or illegal to copy, but the availability of music copying machines and scanners make it easy to copy rather than purchase printed and published versions. This has made it unprofitable for publishers to keep in print any but the most commercially viable publications, and the bad news is that music scores that used to fill the racks of music stores are becoming scarce and often difficult to find.

Similarly, music stores once were a source of hours of pleasure. Pianists of every level of ability would browse the shelves, building a personal library of repertoire. Most of these stores have disappeared, and the few that remain in business stock mostly the standard repertoire that is sure to sell, an unfortunate consequence of the computer and copier revolution.

What repertoire should a pianist study? Whatever repertoire the pianist wants to learn! Repertoire can loosely be divided into categories such as exercises, technical studies, and music to play. Other ways to categorize repertoire include period labels such as *BAROQUE, MODERN, CLASSICAL, CONTEMPORRY, JAZZ, POPULAR SONGS,* or *CONTEMPORARY STYLINGS.* A popular and growing style of piano repertoire is *CONTEMPORARY CHRISTIAN* music, with compositions ranging in difficulty from big note to virtuosic.

Another way of organizing piano repertoire is by genre. Some of these genres are called *SONATA* or *SONATINA, CHARACTER* or *DESCRIPTIVE PIECE, ETUDE* or *SUITE.* Composers from almost all periods write for these genres. A song by *SCHUBERT* or by *MICK JAGGER* is still a song. Piano transcriptions of both composers can easily be found.

There are a number of good source books, many annotated, of the standard classical piano repertoire. Almost all of this music is inexpensively available on recording as well. So whether one's inspiration comes from the printed page or from the recording, both are good ways of becoming familiar with what's out there. I know a student who went on a Frederick Rzewski binge. Rzewski is hardly a household name in piano music, but this pianist discovered a recording, fell in love with the music, and learned several of the pieces despite their formidable technical and intellectual challenges.

And that's what it's all about!

Chapter Twenty-Two

Sound Image

Music is about something. Sometimes the title of the piece gives away the story. *MINSTRELS*, a popular piano prelude by Claude Debussy, is a musical portrait of an imaginary American Minstrel Show, complete with sly jazz references to African American musicians. *THE SERPEANT'S KISS*, a brilliant piano rag by the contemporary American composer William Bolcom, describes in sound the story of Adam and Eve and their encounter with the wily Serpeant, replete with slithering snake allusions and shocking musical moral interjections.

Some piano music is less descriptive. A *BALLADE* by Chopin traditionally has a narrative attached to it, but a *WALTZ* or *MAZURKA* begins to approach the idea of music which has allusion to a general mood but no specific story.

Finally, what is one to make of a *SONATA* by Scarlatti or Haydn? What do they mean? How does the pianist make the printed page come alive? It is hard to retell a story when the story is not clear in the narrator's mind.

I believe that all piano music, even music with descriptive titles, exists as a series of *SOUND IMAGES*, ideas expressed in sound. Their meaning is not necessarily expressed through language but through the interplay of sounds—melodies, harmonies, textures, dynamic contrasts.

There is an extensive discipline within philosophy called *SEMIOTICS*, the study of signs. Some of the most familiar examples of these learned semiotic codes are the ubiquitous "Smiley" Face or the Crucifix. These signs convey personal meanings far beyond the language used to describe them.

Similarly, our species seems conditioned to respond to many non-verbal signs in nature. The beauty of a flower and the shape of clouds are two of the natural signs to which most of us have some response.

Music, similarly, is a two-fold kind of semiotic coding of sounds. The printed page invites us to "deconstruct" the symbols into sounds. But more importantly, the sounds themselves exist in our imagination as a kind of semiotic coding whose "meanings" are the result of complex individual experience. Think, for example, of the familiar first motive of Beethoven's *FIFTH SYMPHONY,* the *FUNERAL MARCH* movement of Chopin's *SECOND SONATA,* or Mendelssohn's *WEDDING MARCH.* All are musical icons in our culture and all have different meanings for each of us who hear them.

Our musical experiences begin before birth, and it is the rare child who does not regularly respond to all kinds of sounds and all kinds of music. There is little question that our preference for Bartok or Chinese opera is a matter of experience, not genetics, but there is little question that our genes are coded to respond to sonorous semiotic coding.

SOUND IMAGE suggests to the pianist that she or he invent the way in which they think the sounds in a piece should go together. Loud/soft; fast/slow; melody/harmony: these are some of the ways in which the pianist can organize the sounds that are represented on the page by music notation, notation that is the composer's semiotic coding of his or her sound image. It matters little whether the pianist's sound image is precisely that of the composer. It matters greatly if the pianist has no sound image on which to base a performance.

What does the piece mean to you in terms of sounds? It's fine to tell a story, using words, but piano music is about sounds, not words. Try to imagine the composition with all its details from start to finish. In your mind, how do you want the piece to sound? That's *SOUND IMAGE.*

Inventing these "ideas" is one of the most creative things about playing the piano. In a real sense, the pianist creates the music each time she or he plays it. You need to tell the "story" each time you play the piece, and that story is a retelling of the "ideas" that you've developed as you learned the piece.

Given an open mind, persons can learn to respond positively to most kinds of music they hear repeatedly. From these sound experiences comes a repertoire of *SOUND IMAGES*. This is an argument for listening to a great deal of music in many different styles from many different periods.

There is a universe of "music" to be heard, experienced, explored, and created, and the piano is in some sense the ideal instrument with which to carry out this exploration. *SOUND IMAGE* is what happens when your imagination is captured by this magic.

Chapter Twenty-Three

Teachers: An Autobiography

MRS. HALL

Mrs. Hall lived in a gracious home on a tree-lined street in Freehold, New Jersey, an idyllic setting in 1947 or 1948 when I began my formal piano study.

My parents had a spinet piano in the living room and in some mysterious fashion, I began playing it when I was barely big enough to crawl up on the bench. I know I could read music by the age of five. I'm not sure how I learned.

My mother's family was quite musical. My maternal grandfather for whom I am named, was a violin student in Russia. After immigrating to the United States and marrying, the family lived in Brooklyn. Grandpa earned his living in the New York garment industry but spent his free time with music, his lifelong passion. The serious music students in the family—the boys—were taught violin. Two of them—my uncles—were professional violinists.

The girls were taught the piano, rated an inferior instrument from what I can gather from family lore. Several of my aunts taught piano students. There is a story, more or less verified by a cousin, about one aunt who was such a gifted jazz pianist that she was offered a job as a piano-player by the famous bandleader Paul Whiteman, an opportunity that she passed up since no respectable young Jewish woman would be caught dead in such "compromising" work. I do know that this aunt was indeed a terrific pianist. One of the real pleasures at family gatherings was to have her roll up her sleeves and play to the astonishment and admiration of her adoring nephew and everyone else present.

My mother's piano skills were minimal. She was largely self-taught and not particularly interested in music, having grown up in the Bohemian atmosphere of a musician's family. But my father who had no musical background whatsoever, was insistent that the gifted young son should have lessons despite the strain on the family pocketbook. So off I went to meet Mrs. Hall weekly to see "what was what."

I have no memory of what Mrs. Hall might have known about music or piano playing. She had a lovely spacious studio in her home, and I am reasonably sure that one of its features was a Steinway Grand piano, prominently placed. Years later a cellist friend and I played a duo recital in this room, and I can confirm it was a good piano of good vintage and in reasonable playing shape.

Mrs. Hall was a neighborhood piano teacher. Almost every city and town in the United States, however large or small, has persons who teach piano lessons in their home or their private music school. Their training ranges from *NONE AT ALL* to *CONCERT PERFORMER*. Their commitment similarly ranges from "earn a few extra dollars" to "provide a wonderful life experience to young and not so young piano students."

The work of a private piano teacher can be strenuous. Most students can only attend lessons after school or on Saturday. For better or worse, the tradition of the individual piano lesson seems firmly established in the United States, and many teachers thus meet a procession of forty or fifty students weekly, usually at half hour intervals. Keeping track of who's studying what and planning for lessons and other experiences can be draining and sadly, the pay is limited because of the limited hours available for lessons.

I don't know how many students Mrs. Hall taught, nor do I know how well they progressed. I remember her as having a pleasant way of dealing with a child. I think she was serious about music. She invited me (and I invited my cellist friend) to play a recital at her home many years later when I was in college.

Many private piano teachers are also supporters of the local arts community and mainstays of the orchestra, theater, and dance companies which sadly grow fewer and fewer in this age of mass communication. Mrs. Hall belonged to several professional organizations, and sponsored at least one recital for her students each year. We would all get dressed in our best clothes, nervously sit in rows of folding chairs, waiting to perform our short selections to thunderous applause from parents and friends, whatever our transgressions. This is pretty heady stuff for any young person. Those recitals, loved or hated by students, are one of the inducements (or deterrents) to practice and work at the challenging skills that are piano study for a child.

My career as a student of Mrs. Hall didn't last very long. My parents were unhappy with my progress and sought other options. While there were many other piano teachers available locally, a family conference with opinions solicited from uncles and aunts yielded the decision to apply to the Juilliard School Preparatory program. I auditioned, was accepted, and stayed there also for one year before, once again, the teacher proved no match for my strongly held ideas about music and my intransigence toward learning how to do things the acceptable way.

I suspect Mrs. Hall, experienced teacher that she was, must have smiled at losing a gifted young student. It happens to all teachers, and usually for the wrong reasons: stage parents. Young pianists are made, not born, and behind every budding prodigy is a pushy parent, friend or relative who dreams of fostering the career of the next Artur Rubinstein or Emanuel Ax. But no young student can be much better than his or her teacher makes them.

This Mrs. Hall story was to be repeated several times with different teachers in our area, until finally I auditioned for and was accepted by the Manhattan School of Music Preparatory Program. My teacher was to be Verna Brown.

MISS BROWN

Miss Brown is still affectionately remembered by former students as "Brownie," but I doubt any of us had the audacity to use this nickname when she was anywhere near! A middle-aged woman of slight stature and very quiet demeanor, Miss Brown could shrivel you with a raised eyebrow. I'm unaware of her ever raising her voice at me. Her even temper must have been tried on many occasions. .

I was also unaware that she held me in any particular regard until only recently when a friend from that time told me that Miss Brown had a special warm spot in her heart for me. I never knew! In my experience, she treated all her students with the same courtesy, care, and attention.

Miss Brown was a good friend of Janet Schank, the founder of the Manhattan School. Indeed, it was rumored that 'Brownie' had a hand in the School's beginning. She certainly was one of its prominent teachers for many years until her untimely death one weekend when she was visiting friends in New Jersey.

"Brownie" had been a student of Harold Bauer, one of the legendary pianists from the early twentieth century. I don't know how much she could actually play, but she certainly seemed to know the advanced repertoire that I studied. I have tried to imagine that young woman from North Dakota moving to New York at the beginning of the 20th century. It must have been an extraordinary culture shock.

We often had lessons in a studio that featured a small Baldwin grand piano that Mr. Bauer was said to have owned. This studio was in the original Manhattan School building on East 103d Street. That building was abandoned when the School was moved to the West Side to take over the old Juilliard School buildings.

Miss Brown kept an apartment on the upper West Side in the shadow of the George Washington Bridge, and occasionally, I would have a lesson there. I was too unthinking to pay much attention to the furnishings but remember a good quality piano.

She favored the classic piano composers: lots of Bach, Beethoven, Chopin and many others with the notable exception of Liszt. I never studied a Liszt work with "Brownie." Other students did. While I'm not sure if it was a good idea, I am sure that she wanted to keep my unrestrained fingers and temperament in check as much as possible. I imagine she felt that an unrelieved diet of "empty" virtuosity would not be good for an already undisciplined if talented student.

One week I bought her the St. Saens *SECOND CONCERTO* which I had heard somewhere and decided I had to play immediately. She was less than thrilled, and that piece did not get much attention in future lessons.

On yet another occasion, I entered a piano competition in New Jersey "on a lark" and unexpectedly advanced to the finals, playing the Beethoven *THIRD CONCERTO*. Miss Brown was flabbergasted! "How did you do that?" she asked? Since one of the other finalists (and the eventual winner) was also a student of hers, I suspect her innocence was somewhat manufactured for the occasion.

This is not to say that Miss Brown did not find opportunities for me when she felt the time was right. As a high school student, she had me compete in several of the national piano competitions and I always fared well. She arranged many recital opportunities for me including my first really important engagement for the assembled music educators of the state of New Jersey. And one summer day in 1958, she telephoned to tell me to learn the Rachmaninov *SECOND CONCERTO* as I was to be the featured soloist for several concerts with the Manhattan Orchestra. I don't know how she engineered that feat!

Miss Brown's teaching emphasized textual accuracy, somewhat restrained interpretation, and solid musical fundamentals. She did not tell me very much about piano technique. I expect this was partially because I had very strong and accurate fingers, and partially because she had no particular technical system that she advocated. She certainly included all manner of technical exercises—scales, arpeggios, Czerny, Clementi, and Chopin—as a regular weekly diet. But the actual development of physical gestures was not part of her teaching, at least with me. As a consequence, I remained innocent of some of the fundamental physical gestures that help a pianist play, and it was not until several teachers later that these became part of my pianistic mechanism.

In all fairness to Miss Brown, I never asked, and didn't seem to need this kind of advice. If anything, I played everything too loud, too fast, too extravagantly, and much of her efforts were taken up in trying to curb my youthful impetuosity and unrefined excesses. I learned new music quickly, and consequently never needed to discipline myself to the kinds of piano study habits that others acquired. In many respects, playing the piano was too easy for me and Miss Brown, despite her best efforts, was never able to satisfactorily channel my abilities to my best advantage. I guess I always knew, somehow, that I could get away with most anything as a pianist, at least at that time.

When I reached my late teen years, I felt I had outgrown "Brownie" and wanted to move on to one of the famous piano virtuosos who taught at the Manhattan School. Miss Brown always said "Not yet!" and somehow, I never pushed the issue. Than, without warning, she died of a stroke on that weekend in New Jersey and I was suddenly without the person who had guided me during the formative stages of my young career.

My fellow students and I were devastated. Her funeral was at one of Manhattan's larger churches and I remember it being almost filled. She had been an institution at the Manhattan School, beloved by generations of students, friends, and colleagues. Like the best in the profession, this unassuming pianist from North Dakota changed lives.

ROBERT

Robert Goldsand was a genuine star, a virtuoso of the first order, with an international concert career and respected management. He appeared with the New York Philharmonic, gave highly acclaimed solo recitals, and traveled the world as a touring concert pianist.

Mr. Goldsand was one of the Manhattan School's big names. He and his wife had managed to leave Austria after the Anschluss. He once told me that they had remained in a hotel room for several weeks, awaiting their visas and safe passage out of the country after the Nazi's made it unsafe for Jews to be on the streets.

It is hard to imagine Mr. Goldsand as Jewish. I have a Columbia Artists Catalogue from the early thirties in which he is prominently featured, a young, astonishingly handsome blond Aryan type from Austria. He had studied with Moritz Rosenthal and thus claimed direct connection with the golden age of nineteenth century pianists and pianism.

Robert was an astonishing pianist. I believe he had a photographic memory for music. He could play any of the Chopin *ETUDES* at a moment's notice, and similarly, would occasionally rattle off one of the Godowsky transcriptions of these works that are unplayable for most of us. My wife Judith, a student of his at the time, related a lesson during which they were choosing a Schubert Sonata for her to study. He seemed to know them all from memory!

On another occasion, he was engaged to play a program of music by Jewish composers in Connecticut. About two weeks before the concert, he was trying to decide what to play, and whether to count Mendelssohn as a "Jewish" composer. My wife and I went to the concert at which he played a program of mostly unfamiliar music by many unknown composers including a work by the contemporary Israeli composer, Paul Ben Haim. He played the entire program from memory, and with an elan and confidence which suggested he had been playing the music for years, not days.

Mr. Goldsand was the original "good guy." A genial man with an enormous intellect, he was exceedingly modest about his accomplishments and seemed never to need to practice. He had a serious back problem, and for many years when I knew him, wore a brace as a relief from back pain. I suspect that some of this came from his method of pianism that was physically quite tense. Despite his mastery of the virtuoso repertoire, I believe Mr. Goldsand was essentially a pianist who emphasized colors, effects, and gestures, and I believe the tension in his arms and body when playing made it difficult for him to achieve these effects, regardless of how clear they were in his mind. To me, Mr. Goldsand's playing was all the more remarkable in that his mastery of his repertoire happened in spite of rather than because of his physical approach to the instrument.

Years later, I had a conversation with a close friend who had studied with Mr. Goldsand for many years beginning in her early teens. She was by this time acknowledged as one of the important teachers of *ALEXANDER TECHNIQUE,* a method of relaxation and release of physical tension embraced by many pianists. I asked her how she had come so far from her earlier training? She laughed and said something like "Are you kidding? All those years of tension and muscle fatigue! I had no other way of continuing as a pianist!"

Sadly, Mr.Goldsand's physical approach to playing the piano did not work for many of us. In our desire to live up to his and our expectations, we practiced a lot, often in physical distress. For many of us, our approach to the piano became mostly tense and physically tight. Strong fingers and finger action, tight wrists, and shoulders, and frequent muscle pain were common.

Tendinitis was a regular part of study. At the time it seemed like a small price to pay for the possibility of pianistic glory. In retrospect, it seems like it was physically the wrong way to go.

I'm sure Mr. Goldsand would have been the first to agree. He was dedicated to his students and their progress, and I suspect he must have been perplexed by the kinds of physical difficulties that beset many of us. The only time I ever had hand problems was within a month of beginning my study with Mr. Goldsand. I attacked a series of double third exercises with a vengeance, vowing to strengthen my fingers and double my technical capacity. Instead, I hurt my hands to such an extent that I had to stop practicing for about six weeks. Today, I know how to do those exercise with no distress and get value rather than pain. Unhappily, Robert never warned me of the possible consequences of doing the exercise wrong. This might have been an oversight on his part. More likely, he was unaware that there was a better way of developing the fingers. Since he, as much as any of us payed the physical price, in retrospect I can only feel sorry for all of us.

J.B.

"How do you practice the octaves?" "Well, I just play them over and over again."

"Do you isolate the fifth fingers, bounce the wrist, shift the hand?" "What are you talking about?"

I had a close version of this conversation with Julian Bern, my wife's former piano teacher from Cornell College, Mount Vernon, Iowa. Mr. Bern was originally from Eastern Europe, a Jewish refugee who spent time working with Alfred Cortot, the legendary French pianist and pedagogue who often took in Jewish refugee piano students after the war. Bern immigrated to the United States and landed in the middle of the Iowa cornfields where he taught a succession of gifted mid-western piano students exceedingly well. In the spring of 1962, he was passing through New York on the way to someplace and invited us to tea at the Plaza hotel where this conversation took place.

We invited Julian to our West Side apartment where he proceeded to demonstrate to me some of the exercises he recommended for mastering the difficult octave passages in the Liszt *SONATA*, a work I had programmed for my upcoming Master's recital but had not yet finished learning. It was a revelation! Rather than simply repeat the passage again and again, he showed me how to understand the physical difficulties and what to do to teach the hand to negotiate them more successfully. I didn't know at the time that he was showing me exercises that Cortot had developed and published in his *RATIONALE PRINCIPLES OF PIANOFORTE TECHNIQUE* and in numerous volumes of piano music that Cortot edited. The revelation was that I was not limited by my innate physical abilities. Even though my technique was naturally formidable, I could help myself enormously and work on areas of weakness, flexibility, voicing, and dynamic in a logical and coherent fashion, rather than the "hit or miss" style which had been my practicing habit since I was a child.

After a few days' discussion, my wife and I resigned our jobs in Manhattan and left for Mount Vernon where I spent not only the summer but a goodly portion of the following year studying with Julian. I learned enough to know that I had a lot to learn, and that there was a lot I could learn, when my draft notice came from the Army and my classical piano education was interrupted for several years.

I will forever be grateful to Julian for that short conversation that told me there was more to studying the piano than "talent" and "mystery," that there was indeed a rational and teachable physicality of playing, and that if I were serious about learning to be a better pianist, I could. My career was not circumscribed by the limits of whatever talent I had. Rather, I could, like the student of chemistry or writing, learn to master the craft of piano playing as well as its art.

SIDNEY

I was discharged from military service in September of 1965 to attend graduate school at Indiana University. After a year of confusion and frustration with the artist-teacher with whom I had chosen to study, I went to play for Sidney Foster late one evening, a last attempt at salvaging a piano career that was essentially going nowhere.

Mr. Foster agreed to take me as a student once I had made the proper political moves to sever my ties with my current teacher. That professor took my departure very badly, and to this day has never again spoken to me, although I was one of his favored students during my year's study with him.

When I finished my degree in the summer of 1971, I asked Sidney why more people did not think and teach as he did. His ideas about both music and piano technique were so carefully thought out, presented, and explained, that it seemed to me only malicious indifference kept everyone from knowing and doing the same. I was a true believer. Sidney said: "People know what they want to know." I have recalled this farewell gift many times since than, and recognize both the truth and sadness of this profound insight. "People know what they want to know." Most of us have too much baggage to be willing to cut to the heart of the matter and be attentive to what needs tending.

Sidney Foster was the first piano instructor in my experience who had a completely thought out method of developing the physical aspect of piano playing. All of his students did similar kinds of exercises and repertoire, chosen to develop ease and flexibility at the keyboard. Sidney held that a pianist's musical ideas were dictated by his or her technical capacity and comfort. Often, an unmusical performance was a performance in which the pianist made compromises necessitated by technical insufficiency. "You can only play as well as you can play." he said, or something like that. That was why he insisted that every pianist learn the technical "craft" of piano playing even before he worried about their artistic development.

I think that Sidney probably hated to teach technique, but did so out of a sense of duty to laying the foundation for all his student's development. It is not coincidental that all of his students play differently, and all play with a sense of ease and comfort that is rare, even today in a more enlightened age. Since many of his former students hold positions in colleges and universities throughout the world, many of his teaching ideas have become widespread. Today, it is a rare graduate piano professor who can simply limit herself or himself to coaching literature as opposed to teaching technique. This was frequently not the case when I studied with Sidney from 1965–1971.

Sidney was really interested in music and the art found in the pianist's repertoire, however. He brought to the study of music the same clarity of thought and understanding that he brought to technique. He was a fabulous pianist, perhaps the greatest Beethoven pianist I have ever heard. He also played Schumann with consummate understanding. Indeed, his repertoire spanned the common practice period and extended well into the twentieth century. He claimed that he had wanted to be a composer but became sidetracked when he won the first-ever Leventritt Piano Competition. He held the rank of Artist-in-Residence at Indiana, and was the first faculty member from the School of Music to receive the rank of Distinguished University Professor. Through his active recruiting, Indiana during this time had one of the most impressive piano faculties in the world, and an enrollment of well over five hundred piano students. Many of the most famous names in the piano business then and now have Indiana connections, and Sidney's influence in all of this was substantial.

I think Sidney found all of this somewhat amusing. A man of diminutive stature, he seemed to know everyone in the music world, and the frequent parties at his elegant Bloomington home were star-studded affairs where students would rub shoulders with the great names of the music world as well as the intellectual world of that great university. None of us knew that Sidney harbored a fatal illness from a very young age, and his tragically premature death in 1977 at the age of 56 left the music world a poorer place.

I would describe Sidney's musical approach as "structural." He always believed the composer, by the arrangement of notes, told you how the piece should go. Discovering the patterns and permutations of the music, and creating a performance out of one's discoveries became an odyssey of musical exploration, an invigorating search for the riddle of the musical story. Coupled with the technical clarity that made playing physically easy, this approach to piano study was like rediscovering the instrument.

The "Foster method" is what I and the myriad of "Fosterkind" have tried to incorporate in our own careers as pianists and teachers.

Sidney was a true original, but there are many great teachers out there, working creatively with the most rudimentary to the most advanced students. It's not always easy to sort out a suitable teacher for oneself: we all have different personalities, strengths, weaknesses, needs. But a good teacher is worth her or his weight in gold, however hard to find.

Chapter Twenty-Four

Theory

When musicians talk about *THEORY,* they are referring to *MUSIC THEORY,* an important discipline within music.

MUSIC THEORY embraces a number of areas: *HISTORY, VOCABULARY, AESTHETICS, ACOUSTICS, NOTATION, MATHEMATICS, TECHNOLOGY.* It is taught in discrete classes from beginning exercises in score (note) reading through advanced and frequently abstract dissertations about musical "structure" and "meaning."

One is never sure whether *MUSIC THEORY* is more a practical than humanistic study: it includes both areas. But since the doctoral degrees in Music Theory are titled *DOCTOR OF PHILOSOPHY* and not *DOCTOR IN APPLIED MUSIC*, more persons seem to side with the emphasis upon its humanities rather than its practical component.

Some of the important vocabulary words that many will recognize as part of theory's language include:

Melody
Harmony
Meter and Rhythm
Texture
Timbre
Structure
Orchestration or Vocastration
Overtones

Some less familiar but equally interesting vocabulary from the discipline of include:

Chromatic Scale
Serial composition
Additive rhythm
Rounded binary form
Schenkerian foreground reduction

It is often observed that music, despite some common international terms, is usually specific to the language that is being used. Unlike science, there is no generally agreed upon vocabulary to describe the same phenomenon in different cultures or countries. Thus a 'Pentatonic Scale' in English is verbally something quite different in Chinese. As the world grows smaller, English designations for musical phenomena seem to be more widespread, but there is still no agreed upon "Universal Dictionary of Musical Terms" to cover the most frequently encountered phenomena.

The best solution for this profligacy of terms is to own a good musical dictionary such as the well regarded *HARVARD DICTIONARY OF MUSIC.* If it's important in music, a reference can be found in this Dictionary. The discussion will, of course, often reference the author's perspective as well as the matter being considered but then, the language of music cannot be reduced to a series of absolute facts as can be attempted with scientific or mathematical formulations.

While some *MUSIC THEORY* is speculative, even abstract, a good deal is quite practical and descriptive. For example, music has cadences, and when a musician understands the concept of cadence and what it implies, a whole new sense of music opens. In this case, the division of large units of structure into smaller units suddenly becomes comprehensible! Thus "Theory" in some sense is a misnomer for this important and practical area of study.

Pianists usually are among the best students in any music theory class and with good reason: their ability to learn and perform music depends upon their understanding of what they are learning and playing. This means a direct application of the concepts being learned in the "Theory" class. Unhappily, for whatever reason, many music students don't always connect how to apply "Theory" to "Practice." This is often the case in the study of many theoretical subjects, but in the case of "Music Theory," there can be no question about the importance of "Theory" to "Practice."

The Piano is played with two hands, two feet, and a "brain." The brain orders the action, the hands and feet carry out the directions. "Theory" represents the "ordering" structured by that brain.

Chapter Twenty-Five

Tone and Voicing

TONE is an acoustical phenomenon that varies with the piano, room, and most importantly, the performer and listener. What is a "beautiful" tone to one pianist is "a hard, percussive, hammered" tone to another. This is another of those words which means different things to different people and is often the subject of heated, occasionally acrimonious debate.

When I was a student, one of the criticisms I often heard was that I played with a "harsh" tone. I spent many years trying to understand what this meant. I experimented with vibrating my finger on the key in the manner of a string player. It gave me the illusion I was doing something, but had absolutely no effect on the sound. I tried various attacks from wrist and finger. Again, there were clearly differences in articulations and in the legato I produced, but the amorphous issue of "tone" remained unresolved, at least in my mind.

In retrospect, the description of my playing as having a "harsh" tone really meant I played too loudly too much of the time with insufficient dynamic variety and contrast, and inattention (unawareness) of voicing the texture.

That might sound like a complicated criticism and it is for the uninitiated, but it is a more complete and accurate description of what some teachers and listeners were missing in my playing at that time. It would have been far more useful to me as a student if someone had given me that sentence as a critique, rather than the vague, somewhat threatening accusation of "harsh" tone. I might have been "beating" the piano, but that's of a different magnitude of activity than "beating one's wife."

At that same time, other teachers and listeners did not find it necessary to mention the "tone" of my playing. They were not focused upon this area or else a different aesthetic concept was at work. Incidentally, today I would agree that I played with a "harsh" tone in those days, but would not leave the issue there. Rather, I would try to be far more specific about what I meant by this catchall summary of sound.

Tone is first of all a product of the instrument and the room in which it is played. Resonance and reverberation are important factors in creating a "warm, rich, tone" or a "dry, harsh percussive tone." "Reverberation time" is a crude measure of the time between when the sound starts and disappears, and is a subject of more complexity than can be discussed here. I like a reverberation time of between 2 and 2.5 seconds in the space in which I am playing. This is rich for some pianists, dry for others. Further, the sound that I hear where I am playing is often quite different than the sound being heard by an audience 50 or 100 feet away. The piano and the room need to have resonant qualities to carry and enrich the sound the piano and I are making, or all my training and efforts are to no avail. A modern auditorium, engineered for amplification and having a reverberation time of under 1.5 seconds, is going to sound "dry" and "cold," regardless of how much I try to adjust my pedal and "voicing."

TONE is also a product of *VOICING*. The piano can play textures of many "voices": four, five or even more sounds at the same time, spread through several different registers. A well-trained pianist can "highlight" one or two of these voices, making them sound more prominent (louder) than the surrounding voices.

"Voicing" is best illustrated by reference to the SATB (Soprano, Alto, Tenor, Bass) organization of a choir. Normally, a balance is sought between the four voice parts. "Balance" here means that the parts are not all sung at the same loudness. Normally, the priority might be Soprano, Bass, Alto and Tenor, with each voice singing somewhat louder or softer than the others in response to a judgment made by the conductor. Indeed, making these adjustments to the vocal "balance" is one of the most important and difficult tasks of the conductor.

Similarly, a pianist who is playing several parts or "voices" needs to balance their importance. Frequently, the pianist seeks the same kind of balance as found in the usual choir model. If one were to consider the outside (fourth and fifth fingers) of the right hand as the "Soprano," the outside (fourth and fifth fingers) of the left hand as the "Bass," and the first, second, and third fingers of the left and right hands respectively as the "Tenor" and "Alto" voices, the pianist will have a good beginning to "voicing" the music.

In my opinion, music is largely "narrative" expressed in sound, and the narrative is frequently found in the "Soprano" voice. Thus, the pianist will often want their voicing to emphasize the notes played by the "Soprano," the outside of the right hand. This is something of a paradox in piano playing. The weakest part of the hand, the fifth and fourth fingers, are usually called upon to play the most important parts of the musical texture, the Soprano and Bass parts. Thus "voicing" at the piano requires attention to the use of the hands and their position on the keyboard. A pianist who is not sensitive to the acoustic realities of "voicing" and the physical ways in which it can be achieved through the hand will almost invariably favor the strong parts of the hand, the "Tenor" and "Alto" parts. The resulting unbalanced textures are often characterized as "Poor Tone" or "Poor Sound Quality."

VOICING is frequently described as a "tone quality" issue. It is, but simply referring to "poor tone quality" is not helpful in understanding or improving this complicated matter. 'Tone" in piano playing is a fundamental issue, whatever the acoustic quality of the instrument and room and the creative use of voicing to achieve more tonal variety and effect is one of the most interesting areas of piano playing. "Good tone quality" and "voicing" are issues that challenge the pianist and her or his sonorous imagination as well as their technical resources and is one of the fundamental ways in which we create expressive performances.

Coda

Someone once said that pianists should play, not talk! There is some truth in this. Music is about music, not about words about music.

Nevertheless, we learn about music and the piano through words as well as through sound, and the words that precede this 'Coda' are an attempt to help us understand what we pianists have learned to hear and to feel.

The world of the piano and its players is changing significantly from that of the nineteenth and twentieth centuries. Economics, culture, and mass communications have helped bring about these changes with dizzying suddenness. I sometimes feel that my generation may be the last to financially be able to work in a tradition that spanned almost three hundred years. Unhappily, this observation is shared by many more astute observers than I, and the viability of the instrument and its practitioners may well be as a kind of museum curiosity commanding less and less attention. I hope this is wrong.

But for those of us privileged to have been pianists, it's been a compelling concert, by turns alternately frustrating, exhilarating, maddening, renewing. There aren't many jobs where you can't wait to get back to work!

And so, in the best traditions of the piano concert, this Dictionary ends with a virtuosic flourish of verbal octaves: "Keep on playin': you'll get it right one of these times!"

Bibliography

Cooke, James Francis. *Great Pianists on Piano Playing: Study Talks with Foremost Virtuosos.* Philadelphia, Pennsylvania: Theodore Presser, 1913.

Dubal, David. *Reflections from the Keyboard.* New York: Summit Books, 1984

Friedberg, Ruth C. *The Complete Pianist: Body, Mind, Synthesis.* Lanham, Maryland and London: Scarecrow Press, Inc., 2002.

Fraser, Alan. *The Craft of Piano Playing: A New Approach to Piano Technique.* Lanham, Maryland and Oxford, 2003.

Friskin, James and Freundlich, Irwin. *Music for the Piano: A Handbook of Concert and Teaching Material from 1580 To 1952.* New York, New York: Dover Publications, Inc., 1973.

Gieseking, Walter and Leimer, Karl. *Piano Technique.* New York, New York. Dover Publications, Inc., 1972.

Good, Edwin M. *Giraffes, Black Dragons and Other Pianos: A Technological History from Cristofori to the Modern Concert Grand.* Stanford, California: Stanford University Press, 1982.

Horowitz, Joseph. *The Ivory Trade.* New York: Summit Books, 1990.

Loesser, Arthur. *Men, Women and Pianos: A Social History.* New York, New York: Simon and Schuster, 1954.

Marcus, Adele. *Great Pianists Speak with Adele Marcus.* Neptune, New Jersey: Paganiniana Publications, Inc., 1979.

Mitchell, Mark. *Virtuosi, A Defense and a (Sometimes Erotic) Celebration of Great Pianists.* Bloomington and Indianapolis: Indiana University Press, 2000.

Neuhaus, Heinrich. *The Art of Piano Playing.* Trans. K. A. Leibovitch. London: Kahn and Averill, 1993.

Noyle, Linda J. *Pianists on Playing: Interviews with Twelve Concert Pianists.* Metuchen, New Jersey and London: The Scarecrow Pess, Inc., 1987.

Oringer, Judith. *Passion for the Piano.* Los Angeles: Jeremy P. Tarcher, Inc., 1983

Parakilas, James et al. *Piano Roles: A New History of the Piano.* New Haven and London: Yale University Press, 2002.

Rosen, Charles. *Piano Notes: The World of The Pianist.* New York, New York: The Free Press, 2002.

Schonberg, Harold C. *The Great Pianists from Mozart to the Present.* New York: Simon and Schuster, 1963.

Schick, Robert D. *The Vengerova System of Piano Playing.* University Park and London: The Pennsylvania State University Press, 1982.